GOODBYE ARGOS

Leo Cahill
with Scott Young

0-7710-9062-5

The Canadian Publishers
McClelland and Stewart Limited
25 Hollinger Road, Toronto

Printed and bound in Canada
by
T. H. Best Printing Company Limited

Contents

"If It Came to a Vote I'd Be Fired"

This was a nice Wednesday evening late in September, when I'd been coaching football for about twenty years; the last six as head coach of the Toronto Argonauts. Our players and coaches jostled around me as I walked up the steps from the dressing room into the clear mild night, with a little south-east breeze blowing off Lake Ontario. This sense of adrenalin flowing, eager tension, I'd felt for football ever since I was a kid. The team was in trouble, I knew that. But that didn't stop me from having a good feeling of hope as the music played and the roar came out to greet the team from the sellout crowd packing the stands skyward all around.

Usually my wife, Shirley, was in the crowd but tonight she was away in the mid-west U.S. visiting her sister, who was ill. Our baby, Betty Lynn, was with her. Our oldest son, Steve, was at North Bay in school, Scollard Hall, but I knew he'd be listening for the scores. Our oldest daughter, Christy, 14, was in the stands. Terry, 13, was around the bench, a treat I sometimes allowed him. Our other daughter, Lisa, 9, who had been born in Montreal when I coached there, was home with a sitter. I thought of them all, just a flash of a thought. They'd been taking quite a bit of razz all season. Maybe tonight could turn it around. When the kids got into schoolyard arguments, the other kids would yell, "Yah, Cahill, your dad's a lousy coach! He's going to be fired!" The other kids would get that stuff from their parents, I guess, or from stories in the press and in broadcasts. Rumors about me being fired had started after our third game, nursed along by my real great buddy, John Barrow, the general manager, as well as by some of the club's board of directors. Even one of the few directors who knew something about football, Johnny F. Bassett, had said a week before that if it came to a democratic vote I'd be fired. The only thing stopping it, he said was, "the old man" – his father, John Bassett, who had financial and every other control of the football club. When you get the general manager buying beer for some sportswriters and criticizing me behind my back and then going out and scouting other coaches for my job (which he denied but was doing, all right), a public belief is built up and nurtured. My wife and kids got it as hard as I did.

Still, another night, another game. Another chance. We'd prepared efficiently for the game against the British Columbia Lions. The big crowd was pretty near delirious, the way football fans get when things have been going wrong and suddenly look as if they're going right. We'd had a bad string of injuries. In their saner moments, the fans did allow us that. Our quarterback, Joe Theismann, was still out nursing the leg he'd broken in the first game of the season. So were five or six other regulars. But Dave Cranmer, our slotback, had come back that night for his first game since serious abdominal surgery. This meant we were able to reunite Bill Symons and Leon McQuay as running backs. McQuay had had a bad leg in the early part of the season but was fit now, if he could get his confidence back with a couple of good runs. Their running had been big when we won the Eastern championship the year before. With Symons, McQuay, and Cranmer back together and the great rookie from Michigan State, Eric (The Flea) Allen, at wide receiver, we had an offence that would stand up anywhere. That is the sort of thing that fans bank on.

Right at the start they almost brought the house down. We barged in close enough for a field goal try which Ivan MacMillan missed but which still was good for a single point. The first time Symons carried the ball he ran a sweep around right end for 29 yards. Two plays later McQuay zipped down the middle for 31 yards and a touchdown. When he hit the end zone he jubilantly flung the ball in the air. His delight was catching, his confidence coming strong. The crowd responded with the kind of a roar that showed they believed better days were here.

From then on it was awful. We dropped seven passes that were right in our hands. We had five passes intercepted. We were offside three times offensively and twice defensively – one of those when B.C. was about to punt and give up the ball. One of our guys moved too soon. That was in the third quarter when we were still leading 8-6 (they'd scored two field goals). Now, instead of having to kick, the 5-yard penalty let them keep the ball, first down. A couple of minutes later Don Moorhead fired a pass to Jim Young that went for a 72-yard go-ahead touchdown. Add it up and we made 17 major mistakes in that game. In most games, four are enough to make a team lose.

The crowd began to sing "Goodbye Leo" in the third quarter. Crowds are like that. One guy started to sing and then suddenly it sounded like all 33,135 were singing. To the tune of Goodnight Ladies, they sang *Goodbye Leo, Goodbye Leo, Goodbye Lee-ee-oh, We're Glad to See You Go.*

It was such a frustrating feeling for me. I'm standing there and I've got 32 football players around me, my associate coaches, the trainers, the doctor – but all of a sudden I'm all by myself, because the crowd isn't singing to any of those other people. They are singing to me. I've never felt so alone. It wasn't a cowardly feeling but a feeling of defiance, surprise, resentment. A feeling that I've done my best and I know when we're playing well and when we're playing badly and I know why all these things have happened to us – and why, you people singing, why can't you understand this? When they first began, anger, dismay and, sure, self-justification, filled my head.

I knew when I got the job that Toronto was a tough scene for a coach. There'd been seven before me in 13 years. Before I came Argos were last for five years in a row. So I didn't have much to start with back in 1967. But we'd finished third that first year and made the playoffs, and from then on were a growing power – winning far more than we lost, finishing first, having two 10-4 seasons. I'd always felt that no matter what the management said or did, the fans would understand. They'd be the final judge and jury. I'd given them winning football teams, always in the playoffs, taken them to the Grey Cup for the first time in 19 years, put out the kind of football that sent season ticket sales from less than 14,000 in 1967 to nearly 31,000 in 1972. From season tickets at 41 per cent capacity to 93 per cent capacity in six years meant we must have been doing something right. In most of those years we'd played over our heads. Now when we finally did have the people we could win with we were shot down by injuries; injuries that no coach could help.

I guess what I mean by all this is simply that in all my budgeting, I just hadn't budgeted for 33,000 people to be singing Goodbye Leo, roaring it out with glee.

I couldn't help but wonder what Eagle Keys was thinking, standing across the field at the B.C. bench. I wondered whether he had gone through this before he was fired at Edmonton, and went on to coach Saskatchewan to the Grey Cup. He was having a bad year at B.C., too. I heard later he was upset about the singing. But probably he was damned glad it was for me, not him.

By the end of it, when B.C. had beaten us 23-9, I had recovered a little. Damned if I was going to show anybody what I felt. I walked down the steps and along the corridors into the bleak and barren dressing room area that we called the catacombs. The players were cursing, or quiet. My other coaches (Blackie Johnston, Jim Rountree, Gordon Ackerman, and Bob Gibson) were all looking at me a little sideways to see how I was taking that damned singing of Goodbye Leo.

The reporters arrived. They come in quietly after a loss, stepping gingerly, needing to do their job but showing some understanding of how a losing team feels. Gord Walker of *The Globe* was one of the first. He came right to the point. "What did you think of that Goodbye Leo routine?" he asked.

I was sitting down, untying my shoes, and I looked up at him.

"As long as they're singing Goodbye Leo, they're not out robbing banks," I said.

When it came out in the paper the next day, Gord wrote that I'd said it with composure. Good for me.

My son, Terry, was still around. I didn't talk to him much then but later at home I remembered that when the Goodbye Leo roar had been coming down around my ears, I had looked around for him. For some reason, I had wished in that moment of loneliness that he would come up and put his arm around me. I can't easily explain why I felt that, except that what happened had seemed inhuman. I knew a lot of those people up in the stands were basically decent people when they were in their own homes. I was glad Steve was away at school and hadn't heard it. But I guess I thought that if Terry had come up to me and put his arm around me, the crowd would have seen it and maybe thought, hey, you know, that's a human being down there. Not a monster. A person like us, with a son who loves him.

When we got home I said to Terry, "Where the hell were you when they were singing Goodbye Leo? I looked around for you and I couldn't see you."

He's a slim kid. Good athlete for his age. He looked me in the eye and said, "Dad, I was hiding."

I said, "Well, listen, Terry, next week they might pull the same thing and if they do I want you to come right up alongside me and put your arm around me and we'll face them together." I've always thought I was a tough son-of-a-bitch but I can't explain that feeling.

When I come to think of it, maybe the kids had been prepared better than I was for this kind of thing. Same with my wife, Shirley. Nobody knows a coach's life quite as well as his wife and kids. There are a lot of coaches who stay in one place all their lives, and have a nice family life and don't have the ambition to get to the top and be one of the 35 professional football coaches in the world. But when you live the life I do and take a wife and five kids along with you it can be a pretty traumatic experience for them.

People rarely said anything nasty right to my face. But at school our kids would get it straight. A kid would say, "Your dad thinks he's smart because he's a football coach but we read in the paper that he's going to be fired, yah, yah." Maybe that's normal, because our kids might go out and try to sound important by saying, "My dad's Leo Cahill." They're proud of who I am and the other kids might be a little envious. But it comes both ways. One little girl told our Lisa one day that she'd give anything to have me as her father. So it is sort of give and take but always until now they'd had more to take pride in than to suffer for.

Shirley always had to handle our kids coming home and telling about what some other kid said about me. She'd always explain, "Well, you know that sometimes you say things that hurt other kids and as long as your dad is coaching there are going to be adults who will say things about him, and their kids will pick it up. When they're angry with you they'll reach down and try to say something that will hurt you. Most of the time it will be about your dad and his job. So just put up with it."

Shirley had a whole married life of going out with me for dinner, and having me sit across from her diagramming plays and making notes on personnel changes and things like that. Our vacations were always interrupted by phone calls about football. Even when we went to the beach in the winter for a week or two, there'd be some recruiting going on, and instead of being on the beach with the kids I'd be tied up on the phone, talking football. She didn't like all that, naturally. But I remember very clearly what she said once when things were the toughest that year.

"You're not the greatest husband in the world and certainly not the greatest father in the world because you don't spend enough time at home. But I know one thing for sure, you're the best coach in the world." This was her way of saying that she knew how much of my life – all our lives – went into the game.

To our kids that was all part of normal life; part of a job I had that, even with the jibes, they were proud of. But in this 1972 season, for the first time, they felt very strongly that all was not well with me. They were troubled. The day after that Goodbye Leo routine, they told me that they weren't going to go to school. They'd just made up their minds, they said. I just couldn't make them go, they said. But when it was time for school, they went. In lunch period that day my daughter Christy went in to the cafeteria. She was immediately serenaded by maybe 200 kids. *Goodbye Cahill*, they sang to her. Her reaction was to turn and flee the place, run for home. We turned her around and headed her right back.

The 107-Pound Center, and Friends

Once upon a time I was a skinny 13-year-old working the riverboats along the Illinois in the summers. When the boats stopped near Starved Rock State Park in the river valley southwest of Chicago I was there with soft drinks and ice cream and candy. Sometimes the people on the river excursions were from Chicago. I always asked those ones if they had seen the Chicago Bears play. If they had and would talk about it and answer my questions, any other customer practically had to draw a gun on me to get served.

I weighed about 100 pounds then. The end of each conversation was the same. I would look the customer right in the eye and say, "You think I'll ever grow big enough to play football?"

Some of them would look at me and laugh. But others, maybe having had dreams themselves once, would tell me, "Sure thing, kid. You'll be big enough." Those were the customers I loved.

One reason I got interested in football was my father. In high school he played football and used to go over to see Notre Dame play. One time when I was a little kid, listening through the door when he was talking late at night, I got the idea that it would please him if I became a football player. It doesn't take much sometimes to set a kid in a course for life, and I think this overheard conversation kicked me off. It was natural for me to want to please him. My dad was the most honest, straightforward, respected person I ever met. Right was right and wrong was wrong, and no deviation. Later in football maybe I did some things he wouldn't have liked but whatever became of me it wasn't from lack of a good example, both from him and my mother. When he died in the spring of 1972, I had been at his bedside for two weeks. I guess the worst year of my life started then and I never did recover.

There were four boys in our family. My oldest brother Don, then Joe, then Fran. I was the baby. My mother was pregnant with me when Joe, who was only about four, died of scarlet fever and pneumonia, which was a very rough experience for my parents and I think affected the way our family went from then on. I mean, they treasured the rest of us that much more, which made our lives awfully good.

Pa had been in the oil business for a while. Sometimes my mother would go with him. When the children started to arrive she couldn't, so eventually he came back home to Utica, Illinois, gave up the oil business and went to work at the big Libby Owens Ford Glass plant in Ottawa, Illinois. He started as a laborer and went all the way to assistant plant manager, which was fantastic considering that he never finished high school. He was a very religious man, said the rosary every day, and thought very strongly about his family. He and my mother, I never heard them argue once in my life. Never heard an unkind word said between them.

Utica was probably one of the greatest places in the world for a kid to grow up. About 1,000 people and right in the Illinois Valley where the Illinois River comes down from Chicago, headed toward the Mississippi. There was great hunting when I was a kid – sloughs full of ducks and Canada geese hardly any distance from our home. And the characters. There must have been 50 or 60 guys from the ages of 50 to 80 who weren't married, old Irish types. There was a little wooded patch right behind our house, which was big and white, near the center of town. Almost any day these guys would be loafing around down there. I used to be kind of a favorite because I was polite to them and would listen to their stories. I had one friend there in Utica, Moriarty, who put it about right. He used to say, "They should build a fence around this town and sell tickets."

Worrying if I'd ever be big enough to play football was an

obsession with me. I'd eat all kinds of things to make myself big. One time I even tried to stop going to the toilet so that I'd put on more weight. It was ridiculous but my parents never scoffed. My mother would accomodate me with any food I wanted. Besides all that was going, I'd drink a quart of milk at every meal. And later when I was in high school in LaSalle, six miles away, because of football practice I'd always miss the school bus and have to hitchhike home. By the time I got done with practice it would be 7 o'clock. Then I'd take a shower and walk a mile to where I could hitchhike. I'd usually get a ride from LaSalle to Route 178 about two miles north of Utica. A lot of times I would have to walk that extra two miles, so I'd be getting home sometimes as late as 9 or 10 at night.

I can still remember getting into Utica those nights and running across the canal bridge and across the railroad tracks and jumping the hedge in front of our house and charging up on the front porch. My mother said she could always hear me coming a mile away. She'd have a big dinner ready for me whatever hour I came in and she never complained. After eating and talking a little, telling about all the great tackles I'd made and so on, I'd really be ready for bed. There were two bedrooms downstairs behind the kitchen and three upstairs. I was upstairs. At that time we had a coal furnace, electric stove and so on, but as a young child I remember that like most people in town we had a cook stove in the kitchen, fired with wood and corn cobs. We used to have a cob shed out the back of the house and, when I was real young, the old outhouse was out there too. There were also a few apple trees and pear trees in our yard. My mother is still there, and my bother Don lives about a block away and brother Fran at Dekalb, almost 60 miles away.

Even in those days everything in my life revolved around football. I was 107 pounds when I started going to high school at LaSalle. Later in life it has never bothered me that I didn't look like a football coach. I mean, you put a thousand guys in a room and ask somebody, "Who's the football coach?" and he'd pick somebody who looked like Jim Trimble. Never me.

I'd be dead last. But then I always think back to when I started to high school, at 107 – I wasn't exactly the guy everybody would point to in awe and say, "That must be our football center." But five years later I was playing in the Rose Bowl for Illinois, which isn't bad. Winning a place on that high school team at 107 taught me a lesson that isn't bad, either – I won it because I worked for it. My brother Don taught me how to snap the ball, and I'd practice by the hour. And, eating the way I did, I got up to 128 pounds in my second year, 147 in my third, and by the time I was a senior I weighed 165 and was pretty close to the six feet in height I am now.

My high school coach was Butch Nowak, a big raw-boned guy from Pana in the coal country of southern Illinois. He was like a god to us kids in the Illinois Valley. He had played for Bob Zupke, one of the great names in Illinois football history. And Butch himself had been All-American tackle at Illinois. He worked his way through college. Everything he got was by loyalty, dedication, and hard work. And that's the kind of football he taught. He told us that a football player had to be able to stand pain and come back for more, stronger than ever. He was especially good with young kids. He believed in discipline and he could see right through people. I'll give you an example: he was always very distant to me when I was in high school. He knew that if he gave me any leeway at all, I'd be in his office the next day with my feet up on the desk.

I remember one year he coached the basketball team. We were playing a school, St. Bede, not far from ours, and he pulled me out of the game for something I'd done wrong.

I resented it and showed it. The stands came right down to the floor and everything was very personal. So they not only saw him get sore and take me out but they saw my defiant reaction. He saw it too and didn't waste any time. "Get in, get dressed, and sit in that locker room," he said. "Don't come back out for the rest of the game."

I was very embarrassed. Not sore any more. I kind of whispered to him, "Butch, you're not going to kick me off the floor in front of all these people?"

He said, "You get off the floor right now or I'll personally carry you off the floor." He publicly humiliated me. It was that important to him to let me know that I wasn't going to dictate terms to him on the basketball court.

I learned the lesson. Later on, when I was accused of showing leniency for some of the individualists we had with Toronto Argos, probably the most difficult part of it for me was that all my life I had been hard with people who broke my rules. Butch Nowak got the message to me long ago and part of my M.O. was to get the message to other people the same way, in the most direct and deliberate manner possible. So it was harder on me than on anybody else when I decided I had to change because of special circumstances in cases like Leon McQuay and others we'll come to later.

Butch was also very kind hearted. On Butch's teams, over the years, several kids made the All-State team in Illinois. That meant being one of the top 11 players in the whole state of Illinois, competing with kids from Chicago and other big cities. Some of these kids from our part of the Illinois Valley didn't have the money to go to the All-State football banquet at Champaign or know how to dress or act, never having had the opportunity of other kids to learn about conduct at banquets and other big deals. Out of his own pocket, he'd take a kid down and buy him a shirt and a tie if he needed it to look neat when he was representing our school. Everybody feared Butch. But when you needed him he was always there.

For the four years when I was in high school Butch always called me Louie. I think he never wanted me to believe that I was so important to him that he knew my first name. I can remember one morning in my senior year, after I finished playing football for Butch. It was a Saturday and I was still in bed. My mother came to the bottom of the stairs and called up, "Coach Nowak is here to see you!"

I jumped out of the bed. I couldn't understand what he'd want me for. When I hurried down the stairs, without my hair combed or anything, he was standing there. He put his arm around my shoulder and said, "Well, Louie, you made the

All-State team. I'm proud of you."

So I had the trip down to Champaign with him for the All-State banquet. And that's when the University of Illinois, which is at Champaign, started recruiting me to be a football player for them. Butch, an Illinois grad himself, was real proud that I had made the All-State team and proud again when I decided to go to the University of Illinois. I always wanted as a kid to go to Notre Dame, like most Catholic kids. But for some reason Notre Dame wasn't interested in a 175-pound offensive center and linebacker.

I can remember I showed up for my first practice on August 16, 1946, five weeks before our first game. This was probably the toughest year for any kid to come out of high school wanting to play football because the veterans coming back from the wars wanted to play too. In those days a freshman, instead of being on the freshman team, had to compete for a place on the Varsity team.

I looked around and saw the guys that were there: Alex Agase, who is the head coach now at Purdue, had been an All-American before that; his brother, Lou, who later was to coach Argos; Buddy Young, who had been a great running back was there, from Fleet City where he was a national hero with the service team. Sam Zatkoff, King Kong Florek. Perry Moss, Ruck Steger, Mike Kasap. We had a super bunch of football players.

On that first day, when the coaches called out for the offensive centers to line up, there were 27 of us. I saw these 27 centers trot out and almost all were either upperclassmen in college or veterans from the service. Big, mature men. I was only an 18-year-old kid straight from high school. Still, I had all the confidence. A real inflated opinion of myself. I was sure I was going to wind up as the first-string center.

They were a rough group. Some had just been shot at, been in foxholes and everything else. They had a different attitude than any football team has ever had in college since. They were go-for-broke, hell-for-leather types. On Saturday nights they were ripping places apart. This was a hell of an indoctrination for a kid. I can remember the scrimmages. They were like war. They'd take no prisoners. They'd knock your ass upside down and they wouldn't consider whether you were 18 or 80.

The first week of practice was dedicated to just cutting down this army to a workable group. A coach would say, "Okay, give me a center, give me a couple of guards, get a team together. . . . " They'd point, "You, you, and you." They'd scrimmage for about ten minutes and the coaches would watch to see if there were any football players in the bunch who deserved to work out with the Varsity. Butch Nowak was up in the stands on the day when I finally got my opportunity in this cut-down process. They called for a linebacker. I must have been about the 25th linebacker that had been called. But I know now this was an advantage to me. All the promising looking guys had been called earlier. The guys I was playing against weren't as good as some of the others. I made about ten tackles in a row. At the end Ray Eliot, the head coach, came over to me and said, "What's your name, son?"

He'd been writing to me all year but I didn't stop to think at that time how many he wrote to. I took it as a kind of insult that he didn't even know my name.

I said, "Cahill. Leo Cahill."

"Well, Leo," he said, "I just want you to know that we're going to have you work with the Varsity. You're going to have a great career here at Illinois." He gave me the kind of talk, you know, that he probably gave to everybody.

When I was walking off the field Butch was waiting for me. "Hey, Louie," he said. "What'd the coach say?" I told him. Butch said, "I think you can do it, Louie. You'll show some of these candy-eaters."

The association with this group was a great thing to me. I was so damn eager. At practice, if the coach would say, "Okay, get a tackle in here!" he'd have to knock me down to keep me from getting in at tackle. "Do we have a guard?" I'd jump in at guard. All season, after practice I'd always hang around to meet the coaches. They knew just as sure as they came out of the dressing room at night that I was going to be waiting there to prod them with, "When am I going to get a chance to play? Am I going to get in the next game?" When I look back now, I've seen many kids like myself. A kid like this, although he has great intentions, you know, is really a pain in the ass. Super aggressive. That was me. I guess still is.

Yet I think they all had a certain amount of respect for me. There wasn't much to me but they knew I was going to try. I played a little. Fourth-string. And I can remember I was in a military program one day that December. We had won the Big Ten and had got the Rose Bowl bid. The coaches' offices were across from the armories where I was training this day in the college's R.O.T.C. program. Somebody told me that Coach Eliot wanted to talk to me. He was sitting there behind his desk. "I've got an early Christmas present for you, Leo," he said. "We're going to take you with us to the Rose Bowl." I found out later that Buddy Young, Paul Patterson, Jocko Wren and some of the other guys had spoken to him on my behalf.

They took 44 players. I think I was about the 44th. But it was the greatest thrill of my life to be a member of that group and to end up playing in the Rose Bowl.

That year U.C.L.A. had wanted to play Army and there was a lot of this, "Who the hell is Illinois?" stuff. Some of our guys – one was Alex Agase – went to a luncheon and got very put-down. The whole tone of all the speeches made by people from the coast was that Army might have made a game of it but Illinois would be a walkover. Agase and the others came back mad as hell and got everybody else mad about how those Hollywood football players were selling us short. A real psych job. But it got us all up.

I remember the kick-off. They kicked off I think to Bill Huber, who'd played two All-Star games before but was back in college. He got the ball and ran right over the chests of about four guys from U.C.L.A.

With about six or seven minutes to play, and us leading 45-14 – far ahead, or I never would have got in – one of the assistant coaches, Ross Anderson, came over to me and said,

"Get your helmet. Coach Eliot said to get you in the ball game."

I couldn't find my helmet, I was so nervous. Then I did. I went out there and it was the longest few minutes of my life. I looked up one time at the clock and thought holy gosh, there's still four and a half minutes left. I was playing offensive center. Tommy Stewart was in at quarterback, with first-stringer Perry Moss resting on the bench. I snapped the ball to Tommy too quickly and he fumbled. U.C.L.A. recovered on our five-yard line. We didn't platoon in those days so I stayed in as linebacker. I was scared to death they were going to score and that it would be my fault. I yelled across the line right then, kid that I was, "We might be the fourth-string but you're not going to score on us!" They didn't either. We held them and I made one of the tackles. But it was funny after. Some of the other guys told reporters what I had yelled across the line: "We might be fourth-string but you're not going to score!" It got printed around, including in the *Saturday Evening Post*, which was like the Bible in the U.S. in those days.

My scholarship that year, incidentally, wasn't a full ride like some kids get now. Mine was tuition and a room. No meals, but I had what they called a meal job. I worked in a girls' residence washing dishes. I'd have to hurry from practice at night to get over there and wash dishes. I ate right there where I worked. In a job like that, if you didn't show up for work, you didn't eat. It kind of encouraged a guy to show up for work.

After the Rose Bowl trip, when they finally thought I might be going to be a football player, I was elevated to a better scholarship situation where I didn't have to work for my meals.

I remember I had a letter from Butch Nowak about then, too. Butch died a few years later when I was out of the valley, but he was still around when I was the only high school kid who made the Illinois team that played in the Rose Bowl that year. He was proud of that. I was always happy that I made some little contribution to him. I guess every football man has his memories of people who shaped him. Maybe there are some players now who will think such things about me, good or bad. But I've always considered myself lucky that first I had Butch Nowak as my coach and then Ray Eliot. They both taught me a lot about football and life, both on and off the field.

My second year didn't really count much. In high school I'd always been center on offense and a lineman on defense. At Illinois, in my sophomore year, they made me a guard on offense and a linebacker on defense. In practice before the season started I went in to rush a passer and Lou Levanti, the center I was going around, leg-whipped me. His spikes caught me behind the knee and cut right to the bone. When I was ready again the season was well along so they left me out altogether so as not to use up a year of eligibility to play. The next year, 1948, I wasn't a regular but I played enough to make my letter and I was damn sure I'd be a starter in 1949.

But to give you a little insight into Ray Eliot. . . . When I reported for practice in 1949, I'd been working all summer on a railroad and I was in great shape. I was sure I would be first-string. I walked in there acting like I owned the world. In our lockers they always hung up a jersey whose color told you whether you were first, second, third, or fourth team. Usually the first team would dress in white jerseys, the second team in gold, the third team red, and the fourth team gray. I opened up my locker and I've got a *green* jersey. Well, I was like the guy who finds a horseshoe under the Christmas tree and says, Where's the horse? I said to myself, well, green must be first-string this year. So I'm pulling on my green jersey and I'm looking around at the guys who I *know* are going to be on the first team. They're in white jerseys. And I see the golds and I see the reds. And I find that the greens have taken the place of the grays. Fourth team! I can't believe I'm on fourth team!

I called my father and said, "I don't know what the hell is the matter here. I'm fourth-string!"

He said, "Well, stick it out." He was a great one for fight 'em with your head down, stick it out, do the best job you can and you're going to make it.

I said, "I feel like quitting."

"You never quit anything else you ever did," he said. "You're not going to quit this."

I didn't quit but I was in this upset frame of mind right up to the first game with Iowa State, which at that time was counted an easy game. There was a place about thirty miles away from Champaign called the Allerton Estate, and this millionaire alumnus used to let the football team go down there and spend the Friday night before each game. A big thrill for us corn-fed kids from Illinois. Palatial gardens. Wildfowl all around the place. We'd have a couple of meals there and build up togetherness, away from the city and everything.

So I said to Eliot, "Coach, am I going to go to the Allerton Estate with you?"

I thought maybe he'd say, "Of course you are." And indicate that I'd be playing.

All he said was, sort of grudgingly, "Well, you can come with us out to the Allerton Estate."

I thought, Christ Almighty, this guy is serious. He may not even figure on dressing me for the game. So we went but still he didn't tell me anything.

On the day of the game, for our meeting, Ray Eliot always used to have a certain setup in the meeting room. He'd have the first team sitting in the first row, second team in the second row, third team in the third row, fourth team in the fourth row. The A.O.s (All Others) stood at the back. I was one of the A.O.s.

Eliot was great at building things up to a crescendo. He gave us the talk about we're getting ready for a non-conference game and we've not only got to win for Illinois, we've got to win for the whole conference. There is no way that we could bear the shame of letting a team from out of the league beat us. Building us up. Building us up.

And finally he said "Okay. The starting line up will be . . . . " And he got up to the blackboard. I can still see him. He wrote the names angling upward: Left end, Klimek. He ended up playing with the Cardinals. Left tackle, Ulrich. He played with the Cardinals, too. Then he wrote: Left guard, Cahill.

You should have heard the other guys yell! And here I'm standing back with the A.O.s. He said to me, "All right, Cahill, get up here where you belong!" He knew what he was doing. Right then I could have gone through the door without opening it.

I think he must have talked to Butch Nowak about how to handle me. Before a game he'd go around and put his arm on each guy's shoulder and say, "God bless you. We've got to do it today." But when he'd come to me he'd always slap me on the helmet and say, "I won't say anything to you," and go on to the next guy. It really used to upset me, him showing attention to everyone else but acting as if I didn't need it.

People sometimes have talked about my methods for getting players mentally ready. Some work and some don't. But Eliot was the greatest I ever knew in this line. In his office even the picture on the wall did something – a picture of the first team he ever coached. It made you feel part of something bigger than any individual – a string of great players, great teams. And every year before we played Michigan, Eliot would tell the Mel Brewer story from 1939. Mel Brewer was a kid from Southern Illinois, captain of their football team that year. The week before they played Michigan, Brewer's mother died. I remember the first time I heard the story was in 1946, my first year, with that veteran group. This was before we started getting invited to the Allerton Estate, and we went on the night before the game to the Champaign Country Club. Our meeting room there was big, with a fireplace in it. We ate, talked, and slept together, getting ourselves ready and psyched for the Michigan game. This night we're all quiet, with the firelight shadows darting on the walls and ceiling, you know – what staging! – when Ray Eliot told about something that happened in this room. . . . "In this very room," he said, "a few years ago we were getting ready to play Michigan. When Mel Brewer's mother died, he came to me and told me that he had to go home. He was captain of our football team and we were getting ready to play the great Tom Harmon and men like him and hell, we didn't have any football players anyhow, but Brewer was one of the best. It was the toughest thing in the world for me to tell him, 'Sure, I understand. You go home and be with your family.' Then, on the Friday night before the Michigan game, I was here in this very room with my team. It was dark as it is right now. The flames were playing strange images on the wall. And then suddenly in the corner of the room . . . " and he pointed dramatically to a door . . . "that door swung open and there stood Mel Brewer. And he said, 'My father and I want to tell you, Coach Eliot, and the players, how much we appreciated your consideration on my mother's death. My mother meant an awful lot to me and I certainly hated to leave my family at this time to come back here to play football with her so recently gone, but this is the way she wanted it. *And if you think I came all the way back here to be beat by Michigan, you're crazy!* "

The week before, Illinois had only beaten a small teachers' college 6-0. Now they were getting ready to play Mighty Michigan, renowned throughout the country, led by Tommy Harmon, national champions. But the next day they beat the Michigan team 16-7, and Brewer made many of the big plays.

They didn't deserve to beat Michigan any more than a high school team should beat the Argos. It was one of the greatest all time upsets. Ray Eliot used that story as an example of what you can do if you set your mind to it. That, and a poem called "State of Mind", which had some lines that went, "sooner or later the man who wins is the man who thinks he can."

Times have changed and people are not as open as they once were about things they believe in. Some tend to scoff. I don't know. Maybe I wouldn't try to use that sort of thing myself with pros, mature men. But the core is there, the essence of what makes one man able to raise himself above others.

The Choice Was Jail, or Korea

What I'm going on here is the idea that what I am – or what any individual coach or football player is, for that matter – is practically unknown to the fan. The football fan sees me standing at the sidelines, reads in the newspapers a version of what I've said, sees me in some basically superficial situation on TV, and that's about all. He doesn't know me where I live, a product of some things I've never told anybody until now. Butch Nowak had one view of his little buddy, Louie. I think he passed on some of it to Ray Eliot, or Eliot figured me out for himself. When our Argos presented the game ball one time in 1970 to Ed Harrington, who had just been suspended one game for a forearm smash on a quarterback, it seemed like open defiance of the football commissioner who had handed out the suspension. But there are some guys away back in my past who, if they'd heard about it, would have said, "Yep, that's Leo, all right." Same with the time in 1971 when I pretended on the phone that I was a player's father to snake him right out of the Montreal office, where he was about to sign, and got him back to the Argos.

The truth is, I've always been a pushy guy. And it has backfired on me plenty of times. I'll probably only write this one book in my life. This means I have this one chance to fill in background that you could never possibly see when I was bad-mouthing opposing players from the sidelines, or never could read in any sports pages. So I may as well come clean on a lot

27

of things that made me what I am, or at least indicated what I was going to be.

Like Korea. I've spent a fair amount of time trying to steer sportswriters away from any romantic idea that I was a war hero, even though I did serve in a combat zone. What really happened was that when I enlisted in 1951, two months after the end of my senior year at Illinois, it wasn't because of any great feeling of patriotism or desire to get to Korea. And when I did eventually go there, the decision I had to make was either go to Korea or go to jail for beating hell out of an acting sergeant.

I really joined the Army because of an opportunity I thought I had to coach football at a U.S. Army camp, Fort Sheridan. Two days after I was in the Army a directive came from Washington that, for the first time in history, personnel would be sent out of the continental United States for basic training: specifically, all enlisted personnel who came in between this date and that date. So, on my third day in the Army, instead of looking forward to coaching an Army football team, I was on my way to Hawaii for basic training. Still, I figured that after my basic training, because of my earlier R.O.T.C. time, I would get the chance to come back to the States for Officers Candidate School. This would have delayed the agony about going to Korea. Nobody with much sense wanted to jump into that Korean thing at that time.

It would have gone that way except for something that happened on the last week of our basic training in Hawaii. I was 22 years old, older than most of the other recruits. I was an acting squad leader, under a sergeant who was on my ass all the time. This sergeant was a Mexican-American from California and he really hated my guts because I was a college graduate. It was college boy this and college boy that, every time he spoke to me.

It was real hot this day. We were supposed to be simulating an attack, up in the mountains. When we reached a certain position because of the heat I told my squad to take a rest in the shade, instead of digging foxholes. I told them, "There are a lot of foxholes open in Korea. You don't have to practice to dig a hole."

Then the sergeant came along. I admit now maybe I was wrong. But when he came up to me and said, "How come your guys aren't digging in?" I said, "Oh, I gave them a rest. There's a lot of holes over in Korea."

He was furious. He said, "You're going to get a whole group killed in this goddam war, pulling this kind of a thing!"

My frustration of the last few months erupted. I said, "After basic training is over you and I are going to get together." And when I said it I tapped him on the chest with my finger.

He said, "If you tap me again I'm going to knock your ass off."

All these kids in my squad were around me and I was kind of the older guy. They looked up to me because I'd been a football player and all that.

So I reached up and tapped his chest again. He threw a punch that I could see coming from left field. I just stepped inside of it and I hit him. I caught him a good one alongside the head. He almost wore out rolling down a little hill. When he got to the bottom he got up on one knee. I thought he was going for his entrenching tool or his knife. I took about four steps and went for him feet first and caught him with those G.I. boots right in the chest. He was gone. He just spat blood and rolled over.

Some men from another squad were afraid I was going to kill him. One grabbed me from behind and one from each side. I was marched down the hill and locked up. I was taken before a captain and then our adjutant, a major, saw me the next day. He had been on Okinawa with my older brother, Don, and we'd talked about that. So he knew me that much. That's all that saved me. He told me I'd committed a very serious Army crime. I could get at least six months, maybe more, and then maybe a dishonorable discharge. He said there was one way out. I'd either go to trial, where he said I wouldn't have a chance, or he could put me right away into a draft for Korea.

"What do you want to do?" he asked.

"Go to jail or go to Korea, is that the choice?"

"That's the choice."

"Well," I said, "in that case. I'll take Korea."

Within a few days I was in the combat zone as a medic. I spent seven months in Korea before our whole outfit was moved back to Japan to a rest and recuperation area. And one day I was standing around there when an officer came up to me and said, "You used to play football, Cahill, didn't you?"

I said yes. "Good," he said. "We're going to put together a team and you're going to be the coach."

That was my first training in coaching. It stood me in good stead later. Not many coaches starting out get into the kind of setup I had pushed at me then – gathering players, buying equipment, setting training schedules, figuring out games, putting the whole thing together. I did it all. I had some fun, and learned some football. Coaches came over from the U.S. to conduct clinics. It all helped put in the year I spent in Japan.

When I got out of the service in the spring of 1953, I still didn't know what I wanted to do with my life, except that I had a leaning toward staying in football. I was anxious to get back to Illinois. I'd had a lot of publicity and good times there. Maybe they could use me somewhere in the coaching staff. I went in to see Coach Eliot and he said he thought they could find something for me.

He put me in as a coach with what they called the B team. It was what a pro team would call a taxi squad, made up of players who weren't going to make the Varsity. We had a schedule with B teams from other colleges.

But I was still a little wild in those days.

When I'd been in college, playing football, I hardly every dated or went to a party. Now, back from the service, I tried to make up for a lot of the fun that I hadn't had before. I did some wrong things. One responsibility I had was helping to recruit players – take good prospects to nice restaurants and sign for their dinners. Well, there were guys around who I'd played football with. They were married and broke. I'd take them down for food and a beer or two and sign for them, too. I got in a couple of jackpots by doing that, and lost some of Ray Eliot's confidence, I'm sure.

Another incident didn't help, either. Andy Wodziak, who I had played with, and I were in charge of this B team. We went to play Ohio State's B team the day before our Varsity played Ohio at Columbus. When we got there we stayed at a cheaper hotel down the street from the hotel where our Varsity team stayed. Sort of poor relations. However, we were supposed to stick to Illinois' plays, so that if a player did make it to the big team he'd be able to fit in. But that wasn't exciting enough for me. I put in a whole new offense for the Illinois B team! Stuff that I'd done in Japan with the service teams. That day we sure surprised Woody Hayes, who is still the coach of Ohio State. Surprised Ray Eliot too. Not pleasantly, I'm afraid.

After the game we came back to the hotel. We'd played a good game. And it was the one travelling trip that this B team made, in its role as cannon fodder for the Varsity, and, well, hell. . . . It was time to eat and we were supposed to be held down to a three dollar meal or something like that. When they asked what they could order, I said, "The sky's the limit." They had flaming sword steaks, crepe suzettes, every darn thing you could imagine. Doug Mills, Illinois' athletic director, called me in the following week when he got the bill and said he and Ray Eliot were really disappointed in me. I tried to tell him it was good public relations but they didn't see it that way.

Anyway, soon after that – I wasn't retreating, I was charging – I told Ray, "I want to coach." You know, reward my irresponsibility with a good job. He misinterpreted. Maybe on purpose. Maybe he knew I meant I wanted to coach Varsity football at the University of Illinois. But he acted as if he thought I meant something like a high school coaching job.

Right after that a superintendent of schools from southern

Illinois called Ray and said, "Have you got a guy that can coach our football team?" Ray said, "I've got just the guy." And he sent me a message to go down there and talk to the people.

Well, I wasn't interested in a high school job but I thought I'd go along just for the ride.

When I got there about four or five other guys had been down there that day, all applying for the job. I got the competitive spirit. I really sold myself. I was going to change this and change that. They called Ray back and said, "Hey, this guy is really great. This is the guy we want and we'll hire him. When can he start?"

Ray called me in and said, "Gee, you did a hell of a job there. They're going to hire you. They want you to go right now."

I said, "Ray, I'm not interested in that job. I want to coach college football." He was, and rightly so, upset.

But there was a friend of mine, Red McCarthy, who had been a pro football player. He was coaching a group of kids at Lewis College, at Lockport, Illinois. Red was in the insurance business, very big, and it took most of his time. He asked if I wanted to help him coach. I said I'd love to do that. So for $100 a week (football season only) I went to Lewis College.

That was my first taste of real hard recruiting. We got a lot of kids from Chicago who'd played on Terry Brennan's high school team, before he went to coach at Notre Dame.

Lewis College had a great atmosphere. The team lived on campus and I lived right with them. One element was strong Italian – the Bagettos and Belmontes. The other was Irish – Walsh, Connor and others. On the same football team. And this was where I learned that a team doesn't have to be all one solid unit on and off the field, drinking in the same places and doing the same thing, always. These Irish and Italians hardly talked to each other, off the field. But we kicked the hell out of everybody in games.

I spent 1954 and 1955 there but I was anxious to make more money. I had met Shirley and we got married, but $100 a week during the football season and odd jobs in the off season wasn't enough.

One day Frosty England, athletic director and coach at the University at Toledo, called Red McCarthy and asked if Red would consider going to Toledo with him as line coach. Football was secondary to insurance with Red so he said no. But I had picked up an upstairs phone while he was on downstairs so I'd heard it all.

After he hung up I went down and said, "Red, why don't you let me apply for the job if you don't want it?" He said he'd help if he could. He called Frosty back. Then I got on and said to Frosty, "I'm going to drive over to Toledo to talk to you." He said not to come, he couldn't promise anything, he already had other people in mind. But I got Shirley and we drove over about 250 miles and I sold myself. He gave me the job.

We won some football games in the next couple of years. In fact Toledo never did much for more than ten years after that until they got Chuck Ealey at quarterback. In 1972 he turned pro with Hamilton and is a good one.

I was happy at Toledo, too, but I still wasn't making much money. We were living in an apartment, with one son, Steve, and Shirley pregnant, early in 1958 when I went to the National Coaches' Convention. In front of the hotel I ran into Warren Giese who I'd met away back in Japan at one of the Army's coaching clinics. I admired this guy a lot. He had just got the head coaching job at the University of South Carolina. He'd been Tatum's top assistant for several years at Maryland back when Bernie Faloney, Jack Scarbath, and some other fine players were there. A brilliant guy, one of the most knowledgeable football men in the country.

When we met in front of the hotel, I had a movie camera with me. I asked one of my buddies to take our picture. I still have the film at home. I'm standing there with my arm on his shoulder. There's no sound on the film, of course, but I can tell you what I was saying. I'm telling him, "Coach, if you ever need any help, I'd really like to work with you. I really have a lot of admiration for you."

Well, he didn't fall all over himself hiring me but a few months later he was making some replacements on his staff and I heard about it. I got a couple of other people to phone him on my behalf and then I phoned him. He hired me and I was with him at South Carolina two years, 1958 and 1959. When I went there first, our daughter, Christy, was just getting ready to be born, in Toledo. I was in South Carolina when she was born. It was really a tough thing on both me and Shirley. You want to be together at a time like this. However, we were both young, healthy, excited about making more money, $7,200 a year. And there was another thing. We had always lived in apartments. I thought we could swing a house in South Carolina and we did, our first. It cost me $15,000. I got it for about a thousand down or something. All I could afford. It was really a nice home. I bought it myself without Shirley seeing it but she was very happy about it. In fact, I know she has often wondered since why we ever left there.

I loved the job, too. It is a real experience, to coach in the South. They measure you. They're expecting you to be a smart-ass because you're a Yankee. Once they find out that you're for them and that you're sincere and that you're not a smart-ass Yankee then you solidify some friendships that last forever. It's the same in Canada. A lot of Canadian people say, here's a guy from the States who thinks he's a real hotshot. If you come on that way they identify you with everything bad about the United States. In South Carolina if you come on that way they identify you with everything that's bad about the North.

So we were happy. Terry, our youngest boy, was born there. But then in 1960 Perry Moss got the head coaching job in Montreal. We'd kept in touch with each other off and on since college, when he quarterbacked at Illinois. On our honeymoon we'd gone to Florida on a free trip for two that Shirley's mother had won at a paint store and gave to us. It's the only way we would have gotten there. Moss was coaching at Miami then. We had dinner with him and his wife. Later I'd meet him at conventions or talk with him on the phone on football business when I was coaching in South Carolina and he was head coach at Florida State in Tallahassee.

When he went to Montreal he asked if I'd be interested. I went up for an interview, with no commitment. I liked South Carolina but this was, as it is often in football, the call of the wild. Also at more money – $10,000 a year. I can remember when that plane dropped into Montreal. I was really surprised. I hadn't expected Montreal to be this kind of a place at all. Big, beautiful buildings. People dressed like New Yorkers. No people in big fur coats. No dog sleds or Royal Canadian Mounted Police on horses. Ken Brown, a young guy from Florida who had arrived with Perry as public relations man, came to the airport with Perry to pick me up. We went out to dinner. I loved it all, the French atmosphere, the big city feeling. I thought, this might really be something, this Montreal.

So I was sold. Soon I was in Montreal and Shirley was back in South Carolina selling that house that she really loved. And the most important part of our lives had begun, although I didn't know then the kind of things that would happen, the heartbreak, the near failure – to the point that once I was out of a job, with my rent due and 13 cents in my pocket, and my wife and kids back in the States because I didn't have a job to support them.

Etcheverry, Patterson, and Other Gods

A lot of people wondered, around 1969, 1970 and later, why it was that Sam Etcheverry and I were more than usually competitive, even antagonistic, when I was coaching Toronto Argonauts and he had Montreal Alouettes. It goes right back to 1960, that first year I spent in Montreal as one of Perry Moss's assistants. I'm not blaming Etcheverry especially. Moss is a brilliant guy but at first he had a pretty well total ignorance of the local situation. To Montreal fans, Etcheverry and some of the other veteran Alouettes like Hal Patterson were practically gods. In Perry's first press conference he said he didn't care who a player was, Etcheverry or anybody else, he had to show that he belonged on this football team. The enmity between Moss and some players, especially Etcheverry, started right there and sometimes came out as open defiance. Of course, I was no more inclined than I'd ever been to keeping my mouth shut if I heard something I didn't like. One night on a plane trip when I heard Etcheverry making some real derogatory remarks about Moss, I jumped right in.

"You're supposed to be a leader on this football team," I told him. "And here you are making cracks about the coach, behind his back. You're a real fifth columnist."

He never did like me after that.

In my years with Perry Moss, I was completely loyal to him and we are still close friends. If I hadn't been, maybe Etcheverry and I would get along better now. Sometimes Moss did things that I could see might go wrong. But I had thrown in my lot with him and he never had one minute's worry about where I stood. I think you could say the same about J.I. Albrecht, who came to us later in 1960 as director of player personnel. I'd known J.I. when I was at South Carolina and he was developing into a professional recruiter. Nobody knew more about high school players than he did at that time, especially in the New York-New Jersey area. But he also had a good line on college talent. Football is war to J.I. A military operation, calling for obedience and discipline. At that time J.I. had what he called a future book on potential professional football players. He called me and asked if I thought Moss would be interested in buying the future book, which he sold at about $750 a copy. Since we were brand new and needed instant help, I thought it might be a great idea. When I mentioned it to Moss, he said, "We need a director of player personnel. Can he do it?"

I said, "I think he'd be a hell of a guy."

A little later Moss went to New York to talk to a football player. On the same trip, he talked to J.I. and in the end we didn't buy the future book, we bought J.I. That's how he first came to Canada. He must have made a good impression with Etcheverry and Red O'Quinn because in 1969 when they started running the Montreal club they brought J.I. back as assistant general manager and personnel director. Later, when O'Quinn was fired, J.I. became general manager.

Moss immediately put J.I. on the road to hunt for players. He goes everywhere by bus and cab. He got on a bus and hit the western part of the United States all the way to California. Out of that trip we picked up Teddy Page, Billy Waite, Barry Hansen, and several other good kids. J.I.'s main job at the time was to find U.S. players whose mothers or fathers were Canadian, as those were. Under the rules at that time, anyone like that could play in Canada as a Canadian. J.I. was the trail blazer in finding dual citizens and putting them to work.

Looking back, it is hard to imagine how any football situation could have had more strikes against it at the start. Perry was general manager as well as coach. As a new coach, he naturally didn't know his own players and their capabilities, and knew even less about the opposition he'd face from the other eight teams in the Canadian Football League. Besides trying to catch up on the coaching side, he had heavy responsibilities. He'd be telling people how to lay out offices, dressing rooms, where to put the air conditioners, speaking to hundreds of groups to promote football. At Florida State he'd had ten assistants, or something like that, and here he had only me and Ken Ship on the football side, Ken Brown doing public relations, and J.I. mostly on the road. We used to get to the office at seven o'clock in the morning. Perry, too. We'd never leave before seven at night. In the football season, it would be midnight. All of that would have been hard enough, without the further aggravation that this group of veterans, led by Etcheverry, just wasn't about to go along with a lot of the things that Perry thought had to be done. One other thing: the owner, Ted Workman, had gone very heavily into Moral Rearmament about then. Maybe it was right, for him. But it isn't something anyone, even one as personally likeable as Workman, can force on others. Especially on a football team. Football players may be as moral as anybody but they don't really dig being told to confess what they've done wrong in the past, and be re-born.

So Moss had these overpowering personnel difficulties. He had guys who were almost his own age: Etcheverry, Patterson, people like that. If they didn't want to swing with him, they could go the other way. He had to win them over, and he couldn't. Part of it was that he was new. Part of it was that they'd spent years under an old pro-type coach, Peahead Walker, and Perry Moss was from a college background with very different values. Part of it also was that they were household words in Canadian football, and he was challenging them. Etcheverry, Patterson and some others had practically written the Canadian Football League's record books. Etcheverry at 30, after eight years in Montreal, had the Canadian record for touchdown passes: 174. He had something like 25,-000 yards gained in passes. He'd had 586 yards in one game, 4,723 yards in one season. And here was a new guy in town telling him he still had to prove his right to the job.

Another thing wrong was the physical setup. We had our offices downtown on Mountain Street. That was miles from Jarry Park, where we practiced. We'd work in the office for most of the day and then hustle out to Jarry Park. It meant that a lot of chances for loyalty-building contact with the football team just didn't exist. During one period we had early morning practices. The players we had recruited for tryouts we had staying in hotels and rooming houses on Sherbrooke Street. They had to get up at five in the morning to make early practice. We didn't have a training table, either, so we had them eating at a restaurant – and that was a couple of miles from the practice field. None of this sat well with the veterans and naturally the new guys picked up some of the disaffection from them.

There was one time after we'd lost a game when we called a Sunday afternoon practice that brought on open rebellion. Funny thing, a few years ago when Etcheverry was coaching Montreal he had to call the same kind of a practice, for the same reason – to shake up his club psychologically. I almost wrote him a note to point out how times had changed.

In one of the first games we played, out in Edmonton, we got shellacked by Jackie Parker, one of the all-time greats in Canada, and his team. Right away it was apparent that although we might have put together the most scientifically-organized team in football, we did not have the players who could win. Defense was one of the weakest points. In Canadian football, with the bigger field and the extra man, things have to be done on defense that just aren't natural to U.S. coaches. Darryl Royal at the University of Texas has said that his coaching experience in Canadian football helped him tremendously with defense when he went back to the U.S. But that was something Perry Moss and the rest of us had to learn the hard way. In August of our first season, playing in Toronto, Tobin Rote set a record against us that still stands for the most completed passes in one game: 38, for 524 yards. In another game two months later in Montreal, Ottawa's Ron Stewart carried the ball 15 times for a fantastic total of 287 yards, another record that still stands. He scored four touchdowns that day. Two all-time records, courtesy of the 1960 Montreal defense.

On offense we weren't as bad – quite. Etcheverry never really assimilated Moss's style, though. Mechanically, he was a little slipshod about faking and stuff like that. He could do some things as well as anybody. One was to compete. Another was to throw the football. But he did it his own way. He didn't want to be told, didn't want to practice new techniques, didn't want to be grooved into any new system. That would have been okay if we'd just said, "Okay, Sam, you do it your way." But his way didn't fit at all the sophisticated crossbuck series Perry put in. The clash between the team's playing and coaching sides was all building up.

Etcheverry, however, was devious. He wasn't all that open in his opposition, as if he felt that his own personal stature would enable him to ride it out. I often wondered if he regretted this attitude when he started coaching. It's too bad players don't have a chance to coach before playing. I'm sure it would change their perspective.

Hal Patterson, another of the greatest who ever played in Canada, was different. There was nothing devious about Patterson. He hated Moss with a passion. And Moss idolized Patterson! Moss thought he was one of the greatest people that he ever coached and one of the nicest. Every time he had a chance, he'd tell people that Patterson was the kind of a football player you could win with.

I remember one day Patterson came into the office. He was almost shaking. I don't remember what had caused it but he told me he was quitting because he couldn't stand Moss.

I said, "Look, don't tell me. Go tell him."

So he went into the big back office Moss had, which was really private. Nobody was encouraged to drop in there lightly. When he came out later and left, Moss came to talk to me. He couldn't believe what he'd just heard.

He said, "You know, Patterson hates me."

I said, "Well, he indicates that."

But then Moss rationalized. Maybe, he said, it was natural for a player to dislike his coach but when it came right down to it, loyalty would prevail. I had my own thoughts on that.

Patterson had two big grievances. One was that Canadian players were under-paid. Oddly enough, Moss did more to help Canadian players than any other person up to that time. Patterson's other grievance was that we spent money for foolish things. One thing in particular aggravated him – a siren that we used in practices. Moss had had a tower built. During workouts he'd be on the tower watching. The siren would go off periodically to tell us to change practice routine. Some coaches use a whistle. Perry used a siren. Fifteen minutes for this. Siren. Ten minutes for that. Siren. Five minutes for the next thing. Siren. Patterson complained that we were spending money for stupid towers and sirens instead of paying it to the players. Funny thing was, the siren had been given to Moss. So was the tower. He made some deal with a construction outfit that we would let them in to see a game in return for the free tower. So Patterson's grievances were really badly-based.

But it is something a coach learns – there are a thousand miles between the players' dressing room and the coaches' dressing room. Fears and apprehensions build up easily unless there is regular communication. Of course, in Patterson's case, also, he was very close to Etcheverry.

But there is one thing I want to make clear. In the end Workman got the blame when we traded Etcheverry to Hamilton – or tried to trade him – at the end of that season. Actually, Workman had hardly anything to do with the decision to trade Etcheverry. It was a staff deal, originated by Moss and agreed to by Ken Ship and me, completely.

What happened was that, with all our troubles, we still won five football games that year and finished in third place – partly because Hamilton, which had been in the Grey Cup in 1959, fell flat on its face in 1960. That put us into the semi-final playoff with Ottawa. Watching that game, watching the films later, and adding up other things that had happened that season, we figured that Etcheverry's arm was gone.

He didn't throw any passes in the first half at all. Ottawa must have thought he was under orders to use the running game entirely, for ball control. But that wasn't so. You don't order a passer never to pass. When he did start passing, three or four minutes into the third quarter, once we had somebody so far in the open that he couldn't have missed scoring, but Sam just couldn't get the ball to him. Ottawa won easily, 30-14.

A lot of people thought later that the trade was made because Etcheverry and Moss were in such an untenable personality clash. But a coach is prepared to put up with that kind of situation, if he's getting production from the individual concerned. We had felt earlier that Sam's arm was gone. The Ottawa game proved it. Added to the personality thing, the best thing to do, obviously, was to make a trade if we could. We reached this decision a couple of days after the Ottawa game, and Moss passed it on to the owner, Ted Workman.

Just luckily, or so it seemed at the time, Hamilton had had that bad season. The Hamilton fans were disenchanted with their quarterback, Bernie Faloney. (Proving that it can happen to anybody; Faloney was a real star.) Jake Gaudaur was president and general manager of the Hamilton club then, with Jim Trimble the coach. The talk was around the league about Patterson refusing to play another season for Moss. Gaudaur called Workman on the phone to ask if Patterson would be available in a trade. Workman staggered him by asking, "How would you like Etcheverry, too?"

A few hours later Gaudaur caught a plane for Montreal. That night they met at Workman's home; Gaudaur, Workman, and Perry Moss. The famous trade – or non-trade – that was going to shock Canadian football was agreed upon. We would send them Etcheverry and Patterson in return for Faloney and a promising young Canadian player, Don Paquette. We were enthusiastic, thinking of an end to the constant hassle with Etcheverry and the chance of putting the superlative Faloney, always a fine team player, into our already strong backfield.

But we still hadn't broken the news to the public. That we did on November 9. Perry Moss had made a statement just before the Ottawa game, mainly as a psychological ploy for both Ottawa and Etcheverry, that Etcheverry was "the best quarterback in football and can stay in Montreal as long as he wishes." His only shot was to try to make Ottawa unaware. Now, a few days later, he's announcing the trade – talking about how well Faloney would fit in with George Dixon and Don Clark to make one of the best overall running attacks in the business.

But all that got through to the public that day, really, was two big words: Etcheverry traded!

All hell broke loose. To Montreal, it was earth-shattering. Phone callers threatened to bomb our offices. We had to vacate them for several hours. But the worst thing of all, to me, was that Moss had been scheduled that day to speak at the University of Montreal to some big football function. With all the uproar, he had to go incommunicado. Then some big wheel at the University got on the phone and said, "Somebody has to come here!" A crowd was waiting. I was the sacrificial lamb. There I am, through an interpreter, trying to explain the Etcheverry situation. I don't know if anything I said ever got to the audience. They threw things at me and spat at me. It was a hell of an experience.

Then it turned out that Etcheverry had a no-trade deal with Workman that we didn't know about at all and that Workman seemed to have forgotten. Etcheverry not only refused to go but he accused Workman of breach of contract and declared himself a free agent. That nullified Faloney coming to us. So what happened was that Hamilton kept Faloney and picked up Hal Patterson. We got Don Paquette – but lost Etcheverry, our only quarterback. He went and played a couple of years with the St. Louis Cardinals and proved the point we had in mind: that his arm was gone. He was released after the 1962 season because of the sore arm.

But if the trade had worked we would have wound up as the smart guys, no doubt about that. Patterson and Etcheverry weren't going to be much use to us anyway and Faloney – to go with Dixon and Clark – might have taken us to the Grey Cup.

In fact, after the Etcheverry-Patterson trouble, we had a

pretty good and cohesive operation. Ken Ship left to coach in the States after the first season but Indian Jack Jacobs came in for the next two as backfield coach. He was a tremendous help, popular with the players. I always liked Jake. You wouldn't have to be around him five minutes before you knew exactly what he thought of you. A tough, ornery guy.

I can remember one time when we went down to Granby as part of our program of promoting football throughout Quebec. We were supposed to meet the mayor, sign the golden book at the city hall, and then they were going to give us a little cocktail party before we went into our promotional spiel. Jake never drank. I guess he drank when he was younger and learned not to. Someone came around with wine and said the mayor was meeting some people and would be ten minutes late. So Perry and I had a little glass of wine. Jake didn't. When they came around with the wine the second time and said the mayor was still busy, Jake said, "I'll try one of those wines." They came around the third time and said it would probably be another 45 minutes before the mayor came. Jake said, "You tell that son-of-a-bitch I ain't going to be here." He'd had it. Moss and I laughed until we practically cried.

Jake stayed with the Als two years, even though he never got along all that well with Moss. Jake was an individual. In 1961, he was as frustrated as the rest of us as we went through about 18 quarterbacks, trying to find one to replace Etcheverry, and missed the playoffs. In 1962, Moss and Workman – with the help of a pile of money – got Sandy Stephens from Minnesota and that was a little better. We upset Ottawa in the semi-final but lost to Hamilton in the final. Jacobs quit right after the season was over, which meant he was gone about three months before Perry Moss was fired at the end of January in 1963. I was very sorry. My association with Moss was most fruitful. I learned more football from him than any other coach in my career.

The Moss era is still talked about in Montreal. When he left it put me into one of the toughest situations of my life – trying to cope with Jim Trimble.

Trimble Said He'd Knock
My Teeth Out

When Perry was fired, he endorsed me as his successor. I wanted it. I'd been there through the growth period with him and knew our personnel. My family had adjusted to Montreal and to Canada. That was related to another very practical consideration, especially for Shirley. When a coach is fired, his assistants usually are dropped at the same time so that the new man can pick his own staff. My itch to get the top job was professional. I felt I was ready and that this was the right time and place. Shirley felt that as well but also knew that for me to get the job as head coach at Montreal was one way to be sure we weren't about to pack up and leave again, as we'd been doing every two or three years since we were married.

She and I talked it over. Naturally she is one of the world's leading experts on Leo Edward Cahill, with a lot of insight into what I can do and can't do. She had a warm family background in that middle-European community around Cicero, Illinois, and principles that aren't all that common nowadays. From when we met she had been everything to me that a wife can be. In her support she was right there with my parents; as principled as my dad and with my mother's ability to encourage me in what I wanted the most. When I was a kid and wanted to play ball and I'd say, more hopefully than anything, that it wasn't going to rain that day, mother would be with me all the way. "There's no way it's going to rain," she'd say. Usually it didn't, either, if she said so.

I don't know if I'm saying this clearly, but when I'm making a big decision I like to tell someone I have confidence in and who has confidence in me. I wanted the job. I knew I could handle it. And Shirley believed in me and believed this would happen. Every time a director came to me and told me that I had a good chance, or I heard that Ted Workman was leaning toward me, it just reinforced all this belief around the Cahill home that a big move upward in challenge, prestige and (incidentally) money was about to happen for us.

Then the rumor spread that Jim Trimble was interested. I still hoped. Shirley never lost faith. But with the background he'd had at Hamilton – one Grey Cup and five Eastern championships in six years – he was obviously a very strong candidate. I have a clipping of an interview with me when he was named head coach. I said, "Sure I'm mad I didn't get the job – how would you feel?" That was my attitude but I could see the logic from the standpoint of the Montreal management – that here was a proved head coach, who might do for Montreal what he'd done for Hamilton.

Shirley couldn't be as philosophical. She knew what it meant to me. For the first time in our married life, she interfered. She phoned Workman's home and couldn't get him but talked to Mrs. Workman. She said, "My husband is the one who should have got the job and would have done it best." She was hurt and knew I was hurt and maybe that, along with some womanly intuition, made her say what she said next. "You've got your big-name coach," she said. "You don't know it yet but my husband is going to Toronto as head coach one of these days and he'll come back and he'll beat this football team." As it turned out later when I did go to Toronto with the Argonauts we beat Montreal a lot more often than they beat us.

But when things cooled off a little, we had other decisions to make. So okay, I'd lost out this time. But I did admire Trimble. Working with a coach of his ability and record couldn't do anything but help my football future. "If he'll keep me as an assistant coach, I'm going to stay," I told her.

Then for weeks I just sat around the office, waiting. I was still under contract but that didn't mean anything if he didn't want me. He'd said publicly things like that I'd done a good job and was liked by the players and that maybe he'd like to keep me on the staff. But he made no decision. Every day I'd sit around the office. He'd come in. I'd wait. I understand better now after being a head coach myself. He was going through who was available in the way of assistants and what would be the best way to go.

When he finally came in and asked me if I would remain on the coaching staff, I was happy. Just after he hired me, he came out to my house and picked me up in his car. He did things in a certain way, his own style.

He said, "Well, let's you and I take a ride." He got me to drive. "Let's drive up to the mountains and talk this thing over," he said. So we started up into the Laurentians. He told me about his background and about things that he wanted to accomplish and asked me for my philosophies on different things. Feeling me out. Oddly enough, the only real contact I'd had with him before he came to Montreal had been after a game we played in Hamilton when there was a fracas between big Angelo Mosca and Jim Reynolds, who was a pretty tough cookie. Wouldn't back off from anybody. It looked as if it was going to be a riot. Trimble jumped into it and got pretty involved. I yelled something very derogatory at him and he yelled something back at me. I can remember the following weekend calling him on the phone to apologize. I felt he'd been wrong, but so had I. I think he liked me for admitting I was wrong. Later we'd talked once about me maybe going to join his staff in Hamilton but that had been casual and had come to nothing.

During this day, driving into the mountains, he told me a couple of stories about big decisions in his life and how he'd got down on his knees and sought guidance. And he told me, I remember, that my impression of God and his were two different things. He kind of led me to believe that he had a kind of special pipeline to the Almighty. I became a little bit concerned.

I didn't know if he was for real or not.

But I took the job. Ed Enos, a capable coach, was hired as another assistant. Trimble gave us almost complete responsibility for putting together the play book. He was immersed in the organization of the Alouettes, meeting the right people, making speeches, promoting the product – doing things he felt had suffered in the Moss regime. He didn't really dedicate much time to football. Up until a month before the season started we never even talked about defense. It kind of scared me. I was used to having things down on paper, organized, all procedure well in hand. Then, when the season got close and after leaving so much to me, I felt that all of a sudden he was considering me as some kind of a threat to his security. This was difficult for me to understand, a guy with such a great record having that kind of feeling about an assistant coach.

We had a couple of disagreements on personnel. I can remember him once asking my opinion on a player. After I gave it he shouted, "Do you mean to tell me that I haven't been fair with this player? Do you want me to knock your teeth out?"

Later he changed some of the offense I had planned, putting in a type of attack more like the one he'd used at Hamilton. It wasn't geared at all to our big runners, Clark and Dixon, or to our other personnel. I was apprehensive. But we got through that season anyhow without too many problems. Won six games and made the playoffs but lost in the semi-final to Ottawa.

The next season, 1964, it got worse. I don't know why. There'd be times at night when he'd drive me home. Or nearly home. He lived out in Hudson, Quebec. Shirley and I had a rented house along the way. I can remember once he dropped me off a mile and a half from home, at the side of the road in a rain storm. I had to dash wildly maybe 400 yards to a phone booth to call my wife, who at that time had a very young baby, Lisa Ann, who'd been born in Montreal. She had to drive the mile and a half to pick me up at this phone booth.

He had other ways of upstaging me, too. He'd call up Vince

Lombardi on the phone, or Stormy Bidwell, or some other big name. Then he'd come out and say, "That was Vinny (or Stormy) I was just talking to. It's nice to have good friends like that that can help you." But he was right. When a C.F.L. coach can get a quick high-level assessment of players cut from the N.F.L., he has a jump on other Canadian clubs.

At Joliet in training camp we had another run-in. He became very physical toward me. Threatening.

I can remember telling him, "Coach Trimble, I can't understand why you would say something like that, unless you don't want me on your staff. But if you think that you are scaring me physically, you're not."

I was just perplexed. I wanted our association to be on a more professional basis.

In our first game that year, he prepared with almost a frantic intensity for Hamilton. They'd won the Grey Cup the previous year. He would go over the personnel, over and over and over again. It was like putting all his eggs in one basket. Maybe he was right for that one day. We went out with a real zest for beating Hamilton, and beat them real good, 32-5, on their home field. I remember someone called me and said, "I see you guys beat Hamilton badly," and I said, "Yeah. Look out the window and see if there is a star in the east. This has got to be another miracle. We're not that good." We still weren't using the kind of offense that I felt suited our personnel.

Then we beat Toronto twice. Mainly because they were worse than we were. The fourth game we went back and played Hamilton and this time they hammered us 32-1. Trimble was very hard to live with after that.

Our fifth game was in Regina. Ian MacDonald of the Montreal *Star* was sitting with him on the plane. When we got to Regina, Ian came to my room and said, "Leo, what the hell is the matter between you and Trimble?"

I said, "I don't know. Why?"

He said, "You and Enos were sitting on the plane playing

cards with Willie Lambert. And Trimble said, 'Look at Cahill there, the immaturity of him playing cards with one of the players, taking all his money away from him.' " Ian was partly puzzled and partly fishing for a story, naturally.

We lost the Regina game, 32-0. That meant in two games our offense had scored one point and we'd had 64 against us. Back on the plane going home, Trimble again was sitting with Ian MacDonald. When we got back to Montreal, in the airport Ian said to me, "Come on, we'll get a cab and go home together."

Just then Trimble came up and said, "Leo, I'll give you a ride home."

I said, "Well, Coach, it's out of your way. I'll go with Ian."

He said, "Oh, no, no. You come with me. I'll be glad to give you a ride home." So we got in the car. On the way home he told me, "You're right. We gotta put in more running. I'm going to put you in complete charge of preparation for the next game. We'll make the changes you've been plugging for. Everything is going to be fine."

I got out of the car ten feet tall. Finally we were going to get this thing together.

Then I got a call about seven o'clock the next morning from Ian.

He said, "You know why Trimble wanted to give you a ride home?" I said I didn't.

"When I was sitting with him on the plane, he said to me, 'You know, there is something that has to be done with this football team.' I said, 'What?' And he said, 'There is somebody ruining our football team and I'm going to have to get rid of this guy.' And I said, 'Who is it?' And Trimble said, 'It's Cahill. It's his fault that we're losing.' He was probably afraid I'd repeat that to you."

I was completely dumbfounded. How could Trimble tell me all that stuff that had buoyed me up, right after telling Ian the opposite?

I told Shirley, "I just can't put up with this any more."

She said, "For gosh sakes, remember you've got a contract. And also four kids. We just can't make a stupid move."

I said, "Well, I'm going to do what I have to do."

So I went down to Jarry Park where we were in preparation for our next game, with Edmonton. And I walked in on Trimble.

I said, "Coach, apparently you don't want me on this staff."

He said, "What are you talking about?"

I said, "I just have the feeling that you don't want me. I think the best thing for me to do is just resign."

"Oh, no, no, no." he said. "There is no way that you can resign. Come here now."

And he put his arm around my neck and took me out to the team in the meeting room. "Here, Leo," he said in front of them. "Go through the films with these guys now. Put in that stuff we were talking about. I gotta make some phone calls."

So he left me and just took all I'd said as so much bullshit. He'd just overpowered me.

I can remember George Dixon and some of the guys who were there. Talking about it later, they could remember the clothes I was wearing and everything else. I had a suede jacket on. I went and hung it up in the coaches' room. Then I went through one reel in preparation for the game with Edmonton. But the more I thought the madder I got. Finally I just turned off the projector and kicked the table about half way over, right in front of the whole team. Then I walked in to the coaches' room where Trimble was, grabbed my jacket out of the locker, and said, "Coach, I'm leaving. I'm through."

He said, "No! No! You're just wrought up. I'll be over to your house tonight."

I said, "Don't you ever come to my house, for any reason. I don't ever want to see you again." And I walked out. That was it. I had resigned.

A day or two later Workman called me in and asked me if there was anything that he could do. He volunteered to help me financially. I was too proud to accept it. There I was, in debt, no job, with four kids and a wife, and no income.

And it wasn't over yet. An article came out in a Freoch paper. The headline said: "Cahill's wife says, quit or divorce." I went down there and challenged the sportswriter. He wouldn't tell me who told him that lousy story. So I grabbed him and we went in to see the publisher. I threatened to sue. The publisher was a more reasonable guy. He told the sportswriter to say where he got the story. Turned out he'd got it from somewhere in the Alouette organization.

I've often wondered if the rumble Trimble and Ian Mac-Donald had a year later, after Trimble had been fired in Montreal, stemmed partly from the incident involving me. They started arguing in a Toronto hotel room a couple of nights before the Grey Cup game that year, then went down to the docks. MacDonald, a sportswriter against a big strong man, was beaten up but refused to press charges. Trimble went to the New York Giants a couple of years later.

The real important thing was that I was out of a job. Shirley said, "Let's leave Canada. Let's go home." When word got around I was offered two assistant coaching jobs at colleges in the States. But even though I was broke I was just too proud to go crawling back. So Shirley took the family and went to her mother's, in Cicero, Illinois. We gave up the house. The furniture went into storage. I went to live at the Y.M.C.A. The room cost me $13 a week. I wasn't earning anything. I didn't have any savings. I didn't eat much. Maybe somebody would ask me to their home for dinner. Or I'd meet a guy on the street who I'd known in football and he'd ask me to lunch or dinner. I'd go to my room and get all dressed up and have no money in my pocket but because this guy invited me I knew he was going to buy the meal.

The lowest point came one Sunday morning. I was walking down the street without breakfast and I had 13 cents to my name. On Monday morning I had to pay the $13 for the Y.M. C.A. At my age – hell, in any other business I'd be set by then – I didn't want to call my father or anybody at home and ask for money. I couldn't ask my wife either. She didn't have any. She wasn't even able to pay board to her parents. Somehow, I got through it. I borrowed enough for the rent at the Y. A day or two later, things started to improve. I had a friend in the printing business, Charlie Losey. He knew things were desperate with me. He said he couldn't offer me much but if I wanted a small retainer and a chance to do some things on commission out of his office, I could. I started to sell pens and other small items on a commission basis. After a few months I was building it up a little. I didn't have any overhead, using Charlie's office and Charlie's secretary.

But I hadn't given up on football. After all, it had been my life, right back to when I was selling peanuts on the Illinois River and asking people if they thought I'd ever grow big enough to play.

When head coaching jobs came open, I applied for them. I tried Edmonton. They didn't reply. When Argonauts dropped Nobby Wirkowski after the 1964 season, I wrote an application for that job. A letter came back – it must have been a form letter they sent to known U.S. applicants – saying that I wouldn't be considered because of lack of C.F.L. experience. I scribbled across it that I'd been three and a half years in Montreal and sent it back to Lew Hayman, managing director of the Argos. That was in my mind a little later when I told a reporter that $80,000 a year and a no-cut contract wouldn't entice me back as an assistant in the C.F.L. because they had no status. Nobody ever knew they were there.

He replied, "Yeah, but you've got money. You're doing well in business in Montreal."

I had to laugh. At that time I would have had trouble raising enough money to get weighed.

It was in the spring of 1965 before I began to see that if I kept hammering away I might make enough in business to get my family back together. I missed them more than I can say. I talked it over with Shirley by phone. Then I went and rented an apartment, so they could come back. I signed a lease for six months and arranged to go back to Chicago fairly soon to pick Shirley up and bring her and the kids back in the station wagon.

But before I did, things suddenly began to happen. The previous year Hymie Katz and his brother Willie had bought a football franchise in the Continental League. They made Etcheverry the coach. His nickname was The Rifle and they named the team after him, the Quebec Rifles. They didn't do well, either on the field or at the box office. But rather than fold they decided to move the franchise to Toronto and have a go there, as the Toronto Rifles. They were looking for a coach. Ray Cicia, a former Alouette and a good friend, also was friendly with the Katzes. Ray had worked with me and coached with the Alouettes on a part-time basis. He talked with the Toronto guys who'd bought part of the Rifles and to Hymie Katz, whom I'd met through Ray. Then Ray called me. "Why don't you go over and talk to the people in Toronto and apply for the job?" he said. "I'll set up an interview for you."

So I called Shirley again. It had been a tough time for her. I couldn't have blamed her for being fed up with football or at least fed up with my part in it, and hers.

I told her about the Rifles moving to Toronto. "What would you think if I applied for the coaching job there?" I said. I didn't gild the lily any. The franchise had failed in Montreal and now was going to Toronto, a very sophisticated city. It was a very shot-in-the-dark football operation at best.

She said, "Well, look, you always wanted to be a head coach. This is your opportunity. Talk to the people and hear what they have to say."

I decided to do it on my way back from Chicago with my family all together again. They stayed in a motel in Toronto while I stopped to see about the Rifles' job. That's when I first met some great people – Herb Solway, Henry Sussman, Irwin Pasternak, Buffy Valentine, Rocky Ludwig, Al Eagleson, Mort Goldhar, and others associated wtih the Rifles. They hired me. I was back in football.

I was stuck for six months' rent on the apartment I hadn't

even moved into yet in Montreal. They showed me no mercy. But in a week or two I was almost too busy to worry about it. We rented a townhouse on Rathburn Road in west Toronto, got the furniture out of storage and took stock. I had seven players and about two months to put a football team together.

I can remember driving downtown in the mornings along the Lakeshore, looking at the skyline of Toronto with misgivings. How the hell were the Rifles going to be able to make a mark in this big, well-heeled city? Starting from nothing with a Continental League team. Competing with the Toronto Argonauts. The pro baseball team was fading fast because already Toronto was showing that in sport it wanted major league or nothing. I knew that the only chance we had at all was up to me: to get a team together and win some football games. And incidentally to show that I could coach.

In those first weeks I worked 20 hours a day, mostly on the phone. I was mainly responsible not only for the team but for buying equipment, getting practice space, recruiting players, setting up a training camp. Bob Frewin, a former football writer, was general manager, but he had plenty to do on the promotional side. I'd call everybody I knew in the U.S. college and pro football and ask if they knew any good prospects. When I got to the players themselves, I could offer a few of them (not many) $250 a game, some $200 or some even $100. Two or three from the whole roster got more than $250. We helped them move, helped them find places to live, helped them get jobs. To get good players to cross the border to a foreign (to them) country to play football for that kind of money really took some salesmanship, if I do say it myself.

One of the first needs, of course, was a quarterback. I thought immediately of Bubba Marriott. We'd brought him to Alouettes from the New York Giants, and later let him go. I called him. He was coaching a high school football team in Georgia. I told him it was a chance not only to play but to get pro coaching experience as one of my assistants. In the end, I talked him into moving his family and coming up here. I tried

Milt Crain, who had played for the Alouettes, but couldn't get him the first year. He did come to us in second year. I also wanted an assistant coach with college coaching experience. I though of a good personal friend, Bob Gongola. He'd been a player at the University of Illinois when I came back from Korea and I'd helped get him a job at Furman University in South Carolina as a backfield coach. Later he'd gone as backfield coach to Harvard University. I called him. I gave him the big pitch about our friendship and sharing this challenge with me and in the end talked him into leaving Harvard and coming to the Toronto Rifles. Which was a tough thing to do because he was one of my best friends and the situation was dicey. However, I needed someone close to me that I could trust.

We put together the football team. That year and the next we had some good players. Marriott, Joe Taylor, Leon Mavity, Ed Harrington, Gil Petmanis – the only Canadian – Bob Blakely, Dick Limerick, Allan Ray Aldridge, John Henry Jackson, Bob Petersen, Jim and Charley Leo, Ollie Dunlop. A pudgy guy I'd never even heard of then, Tom Wilkinson. Joe Williams, John Harris, and many more.

I remember the first time I ever saw Williams. I was with Montreal Alouettes then and he was with Winnipeg. We were getting ready to play Winnipeg and on the films Williams made a couple of runs. Don Clark and George Dixon, two of the best running backs in Canada, then with Montreal, marvelled at this guy and the great ability he had and the great moves he had. But for some reason he never quite made it in Winnipeg or later in Ottawa. For the Rifles, he did a sensational job. Two seasons of better than 1,000 yards rushing.

But I'm getting ahead of myself. We put those first Rifles together, played the first year in atrocious surroundings in the old Maple Leaf Stadium and drew as many as 16,000 fans one night, but we didn't do that often enough. Those were some days. We had to skimp on money. We would take a plane the day of the game and fly somewhere, play, get on the plane and fly back. But one thing that really impressed me with the Rifles was the family feeling. The Rifles' owners really had an interest, not only in winning football games but in me and my family, as well as in the players. It made us work that much harder. If we won, we won together. There was something so completely different from what it was later, with the Argonauts' owners. I always got the impression that most of the Argonaut directors were doing me a favor when they talked to me.

Some real funny things happened in those two years with the Rifles. I remember once we went down to play the Wheeling Ironmen, in West Virginia. I always believed that one of the Wheeling coaches or executives set this up. We were fighting for our life to win and start pulling in crowds in Toronto. Bubba Marriott was coming off a broken ankle and was still limping very badly, so we were going to start John Henry Jackson at quarterback. We flew into some place near, took a bus to Wheeling, had our pre-game meal, got to the stadium and went through our pre-game warmup. On the way back to the dressing room to prepare for the game Chuck Dickerson, one of our defensive captains who also helped as line coach, all of a sudden saw two guys grab John Henry Jackson and slam him up against the wall and make him put his hands up. Dickerson went for them and was about ready to flatten them both when one guy turned around. He had a gun and a badge. F.B.I.

The rap was that John Henry Jackson had left the U.S. in 1960, when he was twenty years old, for a tryout with the Argos. He hadn't made the team permanently (he was on and off the roster for years) but he stayed, married and became a Canadian citizen. So he didn't obey a call for induction in Valdosta, Georgia, in 1961, and in 1964 a draft evasion indictment was issued against him.

I didn't know that then. All I knew was that they were arresting our only healthy quarterback. I pleaded with the F.B.I. men for a stay of execution.

"Let the guy play the football game," I said. "I guarantee we'll resolve this thing. He's been living for years in Canada. There must be some explanation."

No dice. They marched him into a car in his football uniform and took him downtown for interrogation. Bubba limped through the game at quarterback and we won. Jackson got back to the field with three minutes left to play. We gave him the game ball.

Another time, we flew into Philadelphia and took a bus to a restaurant. We told the bus driver to take our equipment to the stadium and then come back for us. We ate. But no bus came back. Soon it was 6.30, when we were supposed to be at the field. Somehow the bus driver had got lost on his way back to the restaurant. He never did show up. There weren't enough cabs. We had to hitchhike. One guy with a panel truck took a whole bunch of the players. When we got there, we were just in time. A few minutes later the game would have been forfeited.

Another time, this was in Philadelphia, too, we were playing a game for the division championship. This was in my second year, 1966. Herb Solway, the Toronto lawyer who was one of our directors, had bought champagne to celebrate the championship if we won it. He had it in the dressing room. In the last two minutes of the game we came from behind and scored a touchdown to take the lead. With 77 seconds left, Herb decided that was it. He left the bench and went to the dressing room to open the champagne. We kicked off to them on their 27. They ran two plays and lost seven yards. Third down on their 20.

Bob Broadhead, who later went on to the Cleveland Browns as business manager, was the Philadelphia quarterback. He threw a long pass. Joe Taylor, one of our defensive backs who now plays for Chicago Bears was in a perfect position for the interception. He had his back turned, watching the ball and waiting for it, when Dave Washington, the wide receiver for Philadelphia, came in on his blind side and made the catch.

That made it first down on the 50. Two more plays and they got down to the 30-yard line. There were just seconds left. Maybe one more play. We were in a blitz. But Leon Mavity, our rover back, didn't go on the blitz for some reason and we didn't get the extra pressure on the passer. Near the goal line Washington made a good move on Bobby Morgan, our safety man. Broadhead threw the ball to him in the end zone and they won the football game.

You should have seen Solway's face, in the dressing room. He had the champagne all open. But in about two minutes we whipped it over to the other dressing room and sold it to Philadelphia.

The Argonaut Go-for-Broke Gang

Considering that the Toronto Argonauts didn't even know I was alive, well, and living in Canada late in 1964, I have a lot to thank the Toronto Rifles for. We didn't challenge the Argos at the box office in 1965 but we did win 11 games and lost only three. Argos, who had hired Bob Shaw as head coach were exactly the reverse: three wins, 11 losses. One sports page head-line read: Which team is Brand X? We made a lot of noise, saying we'd be glad to play the Argos for the city championship and things like that. Of course, Argos ignored us. In 1966 we had a lot of injuries but still won nine, tied for the division title and lost it to Philadelphia in a playoff. Argos again were just the reverse: won 5, lost nine, finished last. The comparisons prompted a certain amount of Argo-needling by the press and fans that the Argos couldn't have enjoyed. Still, I was getting ready for my third season with the Rifles, when suddenly, in March of 1967, Bob Shaw quit the Argos and Lew Hayman started hunting for a coach again.

Because of the way they'd rejected me a couple of years before and the somewhat rude scrawl I'd sent Lew Hayman telling him I did have Canadian experience even if he'd never heard of me, I figured I didn't have a chance. Yet the press and broadcasters kept whipping it up with lines like, "Hey, Lew, there's a guy right in town who knows how to win football games." I didn't apply and he didn't call me. But I won't deny that it was on my mind.

Early in April I was in Chicago recruiting for the Rifles. At six o'clock one morning I had a phone call from J.I. Albrecht. He'd left Montreal in 1963 to go to Oakland Raiders in the American Football League as assistant general manager but he still kept in touch with Canadian football. J.I. keeps in touch with everywhere, all the time. "Hey, Leo," he said. "Do you want the Argo job?"

I knew Rifles were having trouble financially. It wasn't even sure they'd last the season. (They didn't.) In the circumstances I thought I showed admirable restraint. I told J.I. the Argo job certainly would be an interesting opportunity.

He read me. "I'm phoning Hayman on something else this morning," J.I. said. "I'm going to tell him he should hire you. When are you going back to Toronto?"

"Later today," I said.

"When you get there, phone Hayman."

I did. Lew said, "Can you come over to my house?" I went over. This was the first time we'd met but I knew all about his record. He arrived in Canada from Syracuse University in 1932, one of the early U.S. football strays in what later became a flood of players and coaches. He started coaching Argos in 1933 and won the Grey Cup that year and again in 1937 and 1938. Then came the war. When he was discharged from the Royal Canadian Air Force, where he'd coached a service team to the Grey Cup, he went to Montreal and organized the Alouettes. He coached them until 1951, winning the Grey Cup in 1949, and was general manager for another three years. Then he sold his interest in that club, moved to Toronto, and in 1957 became a big man in Toronto management. He was the guy that owner John Bassett leaned on most, as I was to see later.

I'd been told that Hayman was a real tough guy. As we sat and talked that first day at his home I felt I'd never had a more frank and honest reception than he gave me. He's a very quiet spoken guy, except at football games. He didn't raise any false hopes. He'd been quoted earlier as favoring Joe Restic, then an assistant at Hamilton and later head coach before he moved to the top football job at Harvard University. But Lew told me, "If I tap you, you're in. There are a few things I have to clear before I tap anybody."

A few days later, he gave me the job. I wanted a three-year contract and he said okay. He called a press conference, on April 20, 1967, to announce it. The Rifles said they wouldn't stand in my way – in fact, made a little crack about being glad they could help out the Argos by providing a good coach. Punch Imlach said once that the day a coach is hired, he is on the road to being fired. I didn't think about that then. We had two months to go before training camp. I now was in charge of a team that for five years in a row had finished last in the East, with the worst record in all of Canadian football over those five years: 19 wins, 51 losses. At that late date, it couldn't be a matter of assembling a team as much as applying a few patches to the one we had.

When I started looking at the films to study personnel, I figured I was faced with a three-year rebuilding proposition to get a really first-class football team. We had (as they say) a nucleus: a young quarterback, Wally Gabler, who hadn't found himself yet; an old one, Eagle Day, who'd been brought in to bail out Gabler the year before and had done it well; some experienced linemen like Danny Nykoluk, Bill Frank, Norm Stoneburgh, Dick Fouts, Walt Balasiuk, and the excellent young Mike Wadsworth; Dave Mann for kicking; Bobby Taylor, Mel Profit, Al Irwin, and a few others who could catch passes; some good defensive halfbacks, including Jim Rountree and Marv Luster; and, to tell the truth, nobody much who could run the ball except Gabler and Bob Swift, then a fullback. Plus maybe a kid who'd arrived from B.C. Lions with Dick Fouts a few months earlier in a winter deal for the rights to Jim Young. Some people said this new kid could run but nobody knew for sure he'd even make the team – Bill Symons.

Lew told me I was free to choose my own assistants but this had a slight rider to it. Gord Ackerman and Blackie Johnston already had been signed to contracts by Bob Shaw. I got the idea Lew would appreciate it if I decided to keep them on. Also, Nobby Wirkowski had come back the previous autumn as director of playing personnel. This hadn't sat well with Shaw, putting a former Argo coach in a position of authority that challenged his. Nobby was no worry to me, though, and often a real help even after he quit us a year later and went to York University as athletic director.

I thought of the weeks I'd spent in Montreal, on the hook while Jim Trimble made up his mind to keep me, so I didn't waste any time. I got Gord and Blackie in individually and talked to them. I'd known Blackie for years. He'd been with Bob Shaw for only a couple of months but Gord Ackerman had been there for the two Shaw years. They both seemed like good guys, with a good knowledge of Canadian football – Gordon with Regina for a couple of years before he came to Toronto, and Blackie five years with B.C. Lions. I didn't know at the time what great, hard-working, loyal guys they would be to work with over the years. That, I found out.

Also, I had the right to hire one more. I went for Steve Sucic. He'd been in Toronto for three years from 1960-62 when Lou Agase was head coach and had stayed on a while with Nobby Wirkowski, the next coach. I'd known both Lou and Steve away back at the University of Illinois. Lou had been a teammate of mine, Steve just ahead of me, a college All-Star twice. He and Lou both coached at Illinois. Most recently, Steve had been head coach of Richmond in the Continental League. When I phoned him he agreed to come.

The football club then had offices in the old Prince George Hotel. They seemed dark and gloomy to me – not only in appearance but in atmosphere, as if life was real, life was earnest, and there was no place for fun and jokes. I told Steve, Blackie, and Gord that this was a new regime, that we were going to run up the shades and let some daylight in around the Argonaut offices and that they were to consider themselves associate coaches, not assistants. Under Shaw, assistants had been under orders to let the head coach do all the talking. I cancelled that.

They could talk to the press if they wished. Although Steve left after that one year because he and his wife wanted to make their permanent home in the U.S., the coaching spirit that first year turned into something of lasting value. When Steve left I brought Jim Rountree off the playing roster to coach. After ten years as an outstanding Argo player, he fitted in perfectly.

So did Bob Gibson, who had a fulltime job in the faculty of physical education at Bowling Green in Ohio. He would help us through training camp and the early months of the season and then when his own college work began he still came up every weekend to help with our games. He made a big contribution not only as a coach but as a guy who knew mid-west football and could help us with recruiting.

In all the time we were together – Sucic, Rountree, Ackerman, Johnston, Gibson, and myself – while like most staffs we had many wild arguments, they were the most loyal group I've ever seen. I've been around coaching staffs all my life. There are always some troublemakers. We lived together, fought together and drank together and visited back and forth at one another's homes. If anyone bumrapped Cahill, they'd fight and if anybody put down those guys I'd fight. That was the beginning and the end of peaceful co-existence in the Argonaut organization. We had trouble with players and trouble with owners but the coaching staff showed a maturity that could have taught all the others a lot of lessons.

The first talk I had with the players, they were working out at the West End Y on a program put together to get them physically ready for training camp. I dropped in on them informally but on purpose. If I was going to win some games with these people, who had been chronic losers, I knew one damn thing – first I had to get them believing in themselves.

I didn't know any of them. I told them what I hoped we could do and how we'd do it. I won't pretend that I gave it to them all at once that first day but I did begin – and developed it later into an outlook that was our central theme as Argos worked and fought their way back into football respectability.

I told them, you're good enough to win. I always told them that, even in the days when they weren't, and when, against some powerhouse teams like Ottawa, it would take a miracle for them to win. We're not going to pussyfoot, I said. When anyone plays the Toronto Argonauts they'd better fasten their chin-straps because we're going to go for broke. We're going to tantalize them on the field and in the papers. We're going to challenge them. You've been a public laughing stock. You've been shot at and missed, and spit at and hit. Now we shoot back. We're going to keep on getting better and better and soon when teams come to our stadium they're going to come worry-ing.

At times later I'd tell them, "If I put you guys in a room with Hamilton or with anybody else, you'd walk out and leave them in a pile; you're physically stronger, you're tougher, you're meaner, you're nastier." Some of them were. Some of them also weren't real good football players. But they had to hold onto something and they grabbed the us-against-them thing.

From the start I thought Argonauts badly needed a sense of stability, an end to the idea that every setback should bring a wholesale change in personnel. The Argo air lifts in situations of duress were a joke in the league every year until the time I got there. The fans never really got a chance to know the players and half the players never felt they should start reading a long book in case they weren't there to finish it. So I told the players that once we selected our team, we'd stick with the personnel we had. In my mind, I hoped to make the playoffs that first year by hook or by crook. Then we could make changes. But we'd make them carefully in the quietness of the winter afternoons, not in a panic during the season.

They played over their heads then and later against superior football teams. We weren't nearly as good as some other teams like Ottawa, but our guys believed in each other and would go for broke, fight, scrap and give 100 per cent. This was particu-larly true of guys like Bill Frank, Bobby Taylor, Marv Luster, and Dick Thornton, who I picked up from Winnipeg less than a month after I got the job. What a Rogues' Gallery! In any other setup they might have raised more problems than they solved but they revelled in this. Bill Frank was from Colorado, six-five, 245, offensive tackle – and he'd gone from B.C. Lions late in 1964 to Dallas, had been cut there in 1965, and had come to Argos. A rough guy, 24 hours a day. Taylor was a completely undisciplined kid from Calgary but you had to love him on game day. Thornton wasn't called Tricky Dick for nothing. He'd devoted his life to being an all-round free spirit but had a rare ability for making big plays. These people were incorrigibles to other coaches. Somebody in Calgary told me that I should be voted coach of the year every year for putting up with some of the guys I had. But we took this and made it our strength.

Even before we went to camp that year we started the process of building around Wally Gabler. He was only 23. He'd done an awful lot of running for his life the previous year. He'd been thrown for losses 34 times for a total of 342 yards. Rex MacLeod of the *Globe* once wrote that Argos offense in 1966 consisted of Gabler galloping in intricate patterns until his pursuers dropped from exhaustion, whereupon Gabler sometimes could make it back to the line of scrimmage. But I didn't fall into the trap of down-grading him on what he'd done under Shaw. I felt that he could compliment my style of football, which was to pass off the running action, threaten the line of scrimmage all the time with the possibility that the quarterback would run. I just hoped to discipline his running so that it was achieving some purpose, instead of simply fleeing from the posses after him.

I wasn't figuring Eagle Day in my quarterback plans. To keep him meant using up one of the 14 non-Canadians we were allowed by league rules and he wasn't suited to the style of football I was planning – where the quarterback had to be a runner, too. Eagle was the drop-back, sprint-out type that never threatened the line of scrimmage with a run. I needed a more versatile backup quarterback, someone who could be a regular at another position. That's where Dick Thornton came in. When I heard he was available from Winnipeg, I knew he was one of the league's best defensive halfbacks but also could do the job at quarterback. He was a winner, a veteran of the big Winnipeg teams that won everything when Bud Grant was coach. We had to give up Billy Van Burkleo, Chip Barrett, and Vic Sanule to get him. A few days before that I'd made another move: traded one of Shaw's key players, Al Ecuyer, to Montreal for Jim Andreotti, a great linebacker, and Ed Learn, a first-rate defensive back.

In those days I classified Andreotti and Marvin Luster on our football team in the same category as Wayne Harris with Calgary. They all have a hitting power that can't be taught. It is an ability to dip and hit through somebody, getting power through body control rather than weight. One night when I was with Montreal and Andreotti with Argos, he hit Don Clark on a quick opening play that nearly ended Clark's whole playing career. Just about tore his head off. Very few people can tackle like that.

It wasn't until we got to training camp that I really started to put my stamp on the Argos. With the Rifles, I'd used an offense based on flanker motion. The idea was simple. We'd line up one way, and the opposition would set up its defenses, and then the flanker would move across the backfield behind the quarterback to hit the line just as the ball was snapped. It was completely foreign to anything that had been known at that time in football. It was designed to give the quarterback, before the ball was snapped, a knowledge of what defense the opposition was using. If they were in zone defense, there wasn't any movement to cover our moving flanker. If they were in man-to-man, there was. With this system the Rifles broke every pro football record for rushing. With the Argos I figured it would be even more useful because in Canadian football we had five backfielders compared to U.S. football's four.

We called it the student body offense. This comes from an

old saying in football. Everyone has a student body end run – you know, where you get everybody in front of the ball carrier but the student body. But with us it was a whole offense. The men in motion could be pass receivers, or blockers, or we could bring the two men in motion and then run opposite the motion, or pass opposite the motion. When the opposition employed slide coverage to compensate there was a real possibility of confusion. Even spreading the defense would give us a better chance to run inside. I felt it was a great ploy at that time because it was totally new to the teams we were playing. The only drawback was that when you are doing these stunt things in football, you are taking away from practise time on basics. A good football team is developed by basic execution and perfection of plays. But we weren't a finished football team. We needed as many tricks as we could possibly put together – anything that would help deceive the opponents. At first the opposition low-rated what we were trying to do, calling it high school football, or whatever. But I think most of their comments were made to try to shame us out of using the thing so that they wouldn't have to face it.

We kept it right through all the time I was with the Argos. We didn't use it as much later when we got stronger and didn't have to rely on so many tricks. But I can remember key games later when we had Joe Theismann and he scored touchdowns by bringing two guys in motion for an end run or a toss play.

Another thing, when we worked this offense in practise all the time, nothing ever bothered our defense. They'd seen every goddam formation and motion that was possible.

Anyhow, it worked from the start. We won three out of four exhibition games. One of these produced the funniest incident I'd been involved in in football up to that time. (There were some that rivalled it, later.) This was in our last exhibition game, in Montreal. We had a big defensive end, six feet five and 262 pounds, named Mario Marianni. This was right at cutdown time and it was between Marianni and someone else as to who was going to stick at the defensive end position. We had to declare our team the following day. In the fourth quarter in Montreal I decided on the sidelines that Mario wasn't going to make the active roster but that we should keep him around in case some other lineman got hurt early in the season.

So I took Mario aside and said, "On one of the last plays of the quarter I want you to go down on the field with an injury. Then we'll be able to put you on the 30-day injury reserve list. That means we can pay you for the next four or five football games and at the end of the 30 days we'll make the final decision."

So Mario, I'll never forget this . . . all of a sudden he went down like overalls at quitting time, right on the football field. They stopped the game. There were sirens and an ambulance and goddam litter bearers. Mert Prophet, our trainer, was the first one out there and when he came back to me on the sidelines he was in a dither.

"I think the guy is really seriously hurt," he said. "Can't move his legs or his back."

I had trouble keeping a straight face. I'd told Mario to make it a back injury because they couldn't tell for sure whether he had one. Nobody could challenge it.

"I think he ought to stay here at the hospital tonight," Mert said. "I ought to stay with him."

I said, "You'd better do that."

They took Mario out on a stretcher and put him in the ambulance and took him to the hospital, with Mert tending to him all the way. And the first thing Mario did when he got to the hospital was jump up off the stretcher and say, "I'm hungry! Get me something to eat!"

When I told Mert what the story was, he never forgave me. After that I always told him first if I was pulling a fast one. The following day we put Mario on the 30-day injury list. He played a little later in the year. Made a marvellous recovery. I'm probably the first Canadian coach who has admitted this kind of a manipulation. But I assure you it is commonplace and the structure of the league and rules encourages trickery.

Coming off winning three exhibition games, we also won the first two games of the season, against Montreal in Toronto and B.C. Lions at Vancouver. We had beefed up our running game with Jim Dillard but still I had a feeling this early success was too good to be true, and it was. We lost the next four. That would have been the situation, in the old Argo teams, where the airlift would come into play. But we had established with the players that we were sticking with them. We didn't panic. And we were improving.

Joe Williams had been cut by Atlanta. When Rifles sold him to Atlanta back in the spring I prudently got him to sign a piece of paper saying that if he was cut he'd come back to them. Now the Rifles were in trouble financially, the league about to take over the franchise, and we bought Williams and Ed Harrington from them for $7,500.

It was an important acquisition. Ed had played both offense and defense for me with the Rifles so that I knew his capabilities, but he was an exceptional offensive guard. The toughest part of a new football team to get organized is the offense so we put him there, although later his real stardom with us was on defense.

Just as important at that time was that we also picked up Tom Wilkinson from the Rifles. In the games we'd lost, Gabler hadn't played well. His performance had tailed away off. Wilkinson was a pudgy guy who never looked much like a quarterback but he was a great leader on the field. He could take charge in the huddle in a way Gabler never did achieve, with Argos. I wasn't giving up on Gabler. He was young and I thought he'd be good. But in the back of my mind I thought that he'd do better if someone was pushing him for the job. The first time we had Wilkinson in the lineup was for a game with Calgary, which had won seven out of nine games that season, the last six in a row. With Wilkinson on the bench, Gabler played his best game of the season. Wilkinson was in for only about ten minutes. He showed in that time that he could play too, if we needed him.

That game was the first strong indication of the team we could become. Our student body offense drove Calgary nuts, even though both Calgary touchdowns came from their defense – on a blocked kick and an intercepted pass. Dillard rushed for 95 yards, Gabler for 67, Joe Williams for 50, Jim Greth for 49, making the ground game so strong that Gabler and Wilkinson didn't have to pass much. Ron Arends and Jim Rountree intercepted passes in the last couple of minutes when we were under heavy pressure from Pete Liske's passing. We won it 22-13, a real upset. That put us in a second-place tie with Ottawa, behind Hamilton, which didn't do our morale any harm.

There might have been something else that affected our spirit for that game, as well. One of the old-guard Argonauts at that time was Norm Stoneburgh, 12 years with the team, All-Eastern center four times, Toronto-born. We hit it off fine in the beginning. Shirley and I bought a home that he had built and his own was only a few blocks away. His kids and ours went to the same school and we went to the same church. I was a guest at his home for dinner. I thought for a while that he would be invaluable to me as a liaison with the rest of the team. He was also immersed in his two or three young businesses that were doing very well. In fact, at training camp he was going to retire from football. We couldn't afford to lose him so I talked him out of it by saying he could have a couple of days a week off during camp to take care of his outside businesses, if he'd stay and play football. But later he was often late to practice and I got the feeling that he was taking advantage of me.

Stoneburgh was basically a good person and a nice guy but he was so used to seeing new coaches, so used to changes, so used to turmoil, that I came to feel that he didn't have any confidence that I, or anybody, could lead this team out of the wilderness. This sort of thing has an effect on a whole team. Players notice things like someone being late for practices, or missing days in training camp and wonder, what's that guy got that I haven't got? But he's old guard, established, and they think maybe he's untouchable.

Then one night on the practice field he didn't pick up a blitzing lineman on our pass protection. I yelled, "Who the hell does that man belong to?" He'd probably had a bad day at the office or something, and he yelled back at me. I went up to him and said that if he didn't clean up his act that he could get his ass off the field. I might have touched him, telling him, but it was certainly not a punch. By the time the story got to the newspapers and to all his personal friends, it was that he and I exchanged blows.

I admit I was damned fed up with him and for the Calgary game I put in John Reykdahl at center all the time Gabler was in. I used Stoney only when Wilkinson was in. Wilkinson got in a good crack about that, the way he does, saying that he was the only player in football with his own personal center. But the important thing was that if any player had resented the privileges Stoney had, that was ended. They'd seen our rhubarb and now he was on the bench for most of the game. So the world was a fair place after all.

But I have to hand it to him. He told the press that we had a happy team, no dissension, that these things happen in football. Then one night in practice I put him in at defensive tackle where he'd never played in his life. He took it with class; the attitude that I'll play anyplace, godammit, you can't make me quit. Ackerman and Sucic worked hard with him at the new position, gave him a lot of confidence and he started a few games there later in the season and played well. The next year there was a bit of a hassle again when he didn't report to training camp and I suspended him. But I didn't want him to end his career that way. After all, the guy played for 12 years and did a pretty good job for Argos. So at his request I lifted the suspension and he went on the retired list. I've often wished that between us there had been a more amicable parting of the ways.

There was only one other player of importance with the Argos who puzzled me something the way Stoneburgh did, in the sense that I never was sure I could count on him. Mel Profit, our tight end. Maybe I'm bumrapping him, but I had him from 1967 until 1972 and that was a long study. Even his earliest pro experience tells you something. He took a big reputation in both basketball and football out of U.C.L.A., was drafted in 1964 by both the L.A. Rams of the N.F.L. and the Kansas City Chiefs of the A.F.L., played a little with the Rams, then with Pittsburgh Steelers. But in 1965 he just refused to report to Steelers again. Toured Europe instead, then tried it at B.C. Argos bought him early in the 1966 season and he played 13 games for Bob Shaw, including some good ones, which meant that I inherited him. Six feet five and a half. 240 pounds. Milton Earle Profit, Jr. Ask anybody about the best Argos in my time and they'll always list Mel Profit, but he wasn't a football coach's cup of tea. You wouldn't think players would like him, either. He never publicly proclaimed this but he gave the impression that he felt football was a game for thugs. I never felt sure that Profit really wanted to play football. Billy Joe Booth of Ottawa busted him up one time pretty bad with a forearm in 1966. Broke his nose or something. Anyway, he never did play as well against Ottawa when he was with me. Also this thing he used to say – that the sportswriters encouraged brutality in football by glorifying all the cheap-shot artists – always led me to believe that he was likely to shy away from getting hit and would prefer to take the path of least resistance. The total contradiction of that is that he would catch the ball in a crowd in really tough situations. He had this great concentration and therefore could make the big play that could win ball games for you. Shy guys don't do that.

On occasion he would go in and knock the hell out of somebody on a block. But it was a misconception that he was a great blocker. He could block if he wanted to but he wasn't consistent. Also he had very little speed. But people always noticed him. He is so big, for one thing, and was so easy to recognize by his long fair hair sticking out of his helmet, that when he'd get open he'd stand out like a white goat on a mountain and when he'd wave his arms it somehow gave an illusion that he was always open and we weren't throwing to him. There was never ever any direction from the coaching staff or anybody else not to throw to Profit. Hell, he was the bread and butter pass receiver. But fans would leave the stadium grumbling, "Profit is always open and they don't throw to him." So there always seemed a bit of edginess in relations between Profit and me in the public eye and the private one as well.

Certain guys just don't ring true as football players. I play it by instinct. To me, Profit was clever and had a great line as far as the media was concerned. Good at projecting himself as being more than a mere football player, interested in world events, the race situation, social problems, and in explaining how we're just useless overpaid football players. Stuff like that. But I never saw that he was doing much about it, except talk. I don't dislike him. I really like him in a certain way; he's a charming guy. Where he lost me was that I felt he was not dedicated, did not love to play. He was using the game as sort of a shelter, I thought. It was difficult for me to understand why the players looked up to him so much. But they did, and so did the fans. One thing I'll give him without the slightest reservation: the one season that he really did seem to want to play, 1971, right from training camp he was a great leader on the team, our captain in performance as well as in name.

But I've drifted quite a distance from that game when we first came together big and beat Calgary, with Gabler at his best and Stoneburgh mostly on the bench.

As it turned out, that win over Calgary gave us enough points to make the playoffs that year – but we didn't know it at the time. Montreal fell apart completely, winning only two games. We kept plugging along. Won another couple of games in October and had some great satisfaction with one that we tied, against Ottawa, 28-28. If they'd won that one, they would have finished the season tied with Hamilton for first place. They were leading 28-27 in the last few seconds of play when Dave Mann tried a field goal from the 32 yard line. If we had gone for a single with a punt, we would have tied it for sure. But a good field goal would win it. A bad one was a different thing. Ottawa put men back in the end zone to kick the ball out of there and save the single point if Mann missed the field goal. He missed. They kicked it out. The ball was bouncing around on the field, the crowd in a wild uproar, when Gabler picked up the loose ball and kicked it back into the end zone again for the point that tied the game.

Bobby Kennedy was in the stands that afternoon as a guest of John Bassett. They'd been friends since the Kennedys used to spend holidays in Quebec when they were kids. My own children were more interested in getting close to Bobby Kennedy than they were in the football game. When we got home they gave me a play-by-play of all his reactions and how excited he became during those last seconds of the game. Of course, it was something he'd never seen before. In U.S. football after the missed field goal the ball would have been dead, the game over.

That was a very large tie for us. Bill Frank, stripping down later, was offended that anybody should be surprised. "We're not patsies any more," he argued vehemently. And Dick Beddoes wrote the next morning, "Drop kick those limp Argo jokes off the end of the wharf. They're a football team."

So we achieved our minimum first-year objective. Made the playoffs. Also, incidentally, we won rushing honors in the East with Symons, Dillard, Gabler, and the rest going for 2,171 yards. Anything can happen in any one game. So when we went to Ottawa for the sudden death semi-final we had hopes. Hopes weren't enough. Ottawa beat us 38-22. Late in the game, Stoneburgh tore the ligaments in his right knee. We were down and I guess out but I wasn't going to admit it until the final whistle. Then I turned around and who is helping Stoney to the dressing room but Dick Fouts. We still needed Fouts.

"Where the hell are you going?" I yelled.

"The hell with it," Fouts said and kept on walking.

I heard later that in the dressing room Stoneburgh had a

little whisky in his bag. He and Fouts drank a toast to the vanished season while play went on outside. I never knew whether it was true or not but Fouts told Dick Beddoes it was. That winter, as soon as I could, I traded Fouts. He wanted to go back to B.C. but I made it Winnipeg. However, Winnipeg obliged him before long and sent him to B.C.

You'd Better Be Right, Said Bassett

Maybe in here I should have a chapter called The Cast of Characters. But the one I think of first wasn't a character in the sense that Mike Blum, who we got in 1968, was a character (playing well, while bitching all the time); or in the sense that Danny Nykoluk with his cigar, his fetish for being first into the park on practice days and his deep conviction even after retirement against admitting that anyone else could ever play his position, was a character; or in the sense that Bill Frank, Mike Eben, Tom Wilkinson, Bobby Taylor, or Dick Thornton were characters. No, sir, this was the one any of us meant when we said, The Man. Not a player but the owner. John Bassett.

When I joined the Argonauts I was taken by Lew Hayman to meet him. It was not a visit so much as an audience, which is his way. His office as publisher and principal owner of *The Toronto Telegram* was big, airy, and pleasant. He is tall, handsome and vigorous – 52 when I met him. On one wall were pictures of Bobby Kennedy. One of John Bassett's habits when talking (he did most of the talking, any time I saw him) was to pace and wave his arms, and at moments of particularly high dramatic content he might pause and put his face a few inches from a Kennedy picture and be silent for as much as a minute or two. Then he would go on, without explanation.

As far as I know, he never had an indefinite idea in his life. If he had an idea, it was definite. He wore power like some men wear a suit and he must have been pretty good at using it. At that time he owned the Argonauts, a large part of Maple Leaf Gardens, the richest private television station in Canada, and the newspaper. Only in the Gardens did he allow a stamp other than his own. But there, too, he was chairman of the board.

Normally, of course, my contact on football matters was not directly with him. I had full charge of personnel, recruiting, signings and trades, operating under Lew Hayman, with a budget that was fairly flexible. If I wanted to give a new player a bonus of more than $20,000 I would have to clear it with Lew Hayman. Same with exceptional salaries. No doubt Lew cleared some matters with Bassett but I was pretty well given my head. If it happened that Bassett didn't agree with what I was doing, I'd often get the message from other sources. Public ones, like sports columns. Security was never very good around the Argos. Sometimes the breaches could only have come from the top. When John Bassett wanted to get a point across either anonymously or openly, he could start with the sports editor of the *Telegram* (there were three in my time), or the sports director of CFTO, Johnny Esaw, who also was sports director of the C.T.V. network, in which Bassett had the strongest voice. Often his word would be only in the form of a suggestion or tip. But when it came from Bassett, a mere opinion had more power than a direct order would have from a lesser man. And if he felt like putting extra heat on, he would phone Milt Dunnell of *The Toronto Star* and let him have it exclusively. This was shrewd. When a man gets headlines in his own paper it might be treated as ho-hum. In the opposition the impact would never be questioned. In that way, he extended his influence to the *Star*, although partly his interest there was respect and admiration for Dunnell, the *Star's* long time sports editor.

His combination of charm, knowledge, conviction, raw power, and media outlets made him a hard man to stand up against in any dispute. He thought he knew more about quarterbacks than any man alive, which is where I came in. I always felt he was about as well versed on Q.B.s as he was on humility.

At first I saw it as no problem that he warmly liked Wally

Gabler. Gabler was a gentleman, intelligent, well brought up, at home in any company. Gabler also was a personal friend of John Bassett's son, Johnny F., a rising man of power in his own right, both in following his father's pursuits and doing things on his own. Gabler at his flashing best had the kind of personal class that the Bassetts liked and admired.

That didn't bother me, originally. He was the quarterback I favored, too, of what I had.

From the beginning, however, I was never quite happy with how Gabler was able to apply his natural ability and intelligence to make the best use of our plays, or assert himself as leader of the football team. With a team of Argo gentlemen like Al Irwin, Mike Eben, Jim Henderson, Mel Profit, and some others he would have been okay. But if it was no secret that Bassett liked and admired Gabler, it was also no secret that our Rogues' Gallery – the ones who accepted the leadership of Bobby Taylor – felt just the opposite.

Taylor just wasn't the silver spoon type. When he was a kid in Calgary, a coach once told him that he'd never be a football player. But he'd built himself into a little giant, at five-ten and 185. He was Argos' leading pass receiver when I came and for two years after that, and had an indomitable drive for extra yards when he caught the ball. He was a pro athlete and wanted nothing else. He told somebody once, "I give a pound of flesh for a pound of gold." He was never sparing with the pounds of flesh but what a guy to deal with!

You had to admire Bobby Taylor's enthusiasm, his toughness. He gave so much of himself that he excited other players, had a great ability to light the flame. But with my temperament, I couldn't look at him all week long without nearly having a nervous breakdown. I found myself looking the other way. If we were in calisthenics doing side-straddle hops and a coach said stand up, Taylor would sit down. If you said go left, Taylor would go right. Not because he was a nasty person. He was mischievous and undisciplined. He had made up his mind that nobody was going to tell him what to do. He once acknowledged publicly that a lot of coaches couldn't have handled the Argos but that I could. "Leo goes along with a lot of things that other coaches wouldn't," he said. He was one of them. I put up for years with Bobby Taylor and his attitudes because he was a good football player and a good leader. But if you had four Bobby Taylors on a football team you just couldn't win. They'd all be doing what they wanted to do. I wish I had a nickel for every time I would come in after practice and scream to the coaches to get rid of that little S.O.B. Then I'd change my mind.

Anyway, Bobby Taylor's idea was that on a good football team the guys have to play together, fight together, drink together. Gabler just isn't that style of guy. And Taylor's reaction to his refusal to join in was typical Taylor of those days. In practice, I've seen Gabler throw an almost perfect pass over Taylor's left shoulder and Taylor wouldn't raise his arms to catch it. He'd let the ball fall right on the ground just because Gabler was throwing the ball. After I brought in Tom Wilkinson from the Rifles, it got worse and stayed that way. Wilkinson would step in to take his turn in the huddle and Taylor would say, "All right, boys, here's our quarterback, Let's go."

That kind of conflict affected Gabler. It had to. It's the kind of pressure that rarely comes to a quarterback – because in most teams if some players were harassing their own quarterback, the coach would reprimand them or get rid of them. But with us, the people against Gabler were also the heart of what we were trying to portray. In that situation Gabler sometimes seemed indecisive in times of stress. It would be a miracle if he hadn't.

However, I kept this feeling about Gabler more or less to myself. In 1968 again we had Tom Wilkinson around for insurance, but he played only 15 or 20 minutes all season. We improved the team in some positions. In training camp we converted fullback Bob Swift to a guard and a couple of years later to a center. Swift didn't like either change a bit but might realize now that as a fullback he'd have been through long ago; as it is, he's been an All-Canadian center and should be good for years yet. In September we picked up Mike Blum as a linebacker. He played well for us, but wasn't any new soul-mate for Gabler. He was rough and tough. In his first game for us in Montreal Coach Kay Dalton spent most of the game yelling at his player, "Get that Number 70!" In his second, he knocked Montreal quarterback Carroll Williams groggy and they feuded throughout the game. In his third, in Winnipeg, Dave Raimey got so sore at him that he grabbed Blum's helmet after the game and whaled Blum with it.

Incidentally, I was learning that the spirit I'd tried so hard to instil couldn't be turned on or off at will. In Vancouver for an exhibition game in July I wanted to a lot of experimenting with new personnel and was prepared to lose a game doing it. We were blasted 46-7. This offended our new-found pride more than a little, especially among the veterans of 1967, including Bill Frank, who had played in B.C. and wanted to look good. After the game, they had a hell of a party out of sheer disgust. I was aware it was going on. I told the rest of the coaches, don't bother them tonight, let them get this out of their system so when we get on the plane tomorrow there won't be any problems. But there was some furniture busted and other rowdiness. Beer bottles thrown out of windows and stuff like that. I got a call at 4 a.m. that my team was relaxing so strenuously that nobody else in the hotel could sleep. We quietened them down and the next day paid the damages and placated the management.

But when the season began and play was in earnest, they delivered. Did so well, in fact, that after one game in Ottawa when I tried to shake hands with Coach Frank Clair, whom I'd always admired, he brushed past me muttering, "Got a bunch of hammers on that football team, dirtiest bunch I ever saw." Left me standing there with my hand out. That cured me for years of trying to shake hands with opposing coaches, win or lose.

We were pretty good right from the start of 1968. By the middle of September we had four wins and three losses, second only to the Ottawa powerhouse, which that year averaged 29.7 points a game. Our 1967 record had been five wins, eight losses and a tie. We improved that to nine wins and five losses in 1968, just two points behind first-place Ottawa and five up on Hamilton. That put us into the Eastern semi-final with Hamilton on Saturday, November 9, one of the most satisfying games I ever coached.

Anybody who has followed Canadian football at all knows the Hamilton folklore. Some of it was real enough. For years they'd always been up there, winning Eastern championships and Grey Cups, the team you had to beat. They humbled the Argonauts often enough through the years, including in 1961 when in the two-game total points Eastern final Hamilton lost the first 25-7 but won the second 48-2 to take the round and get into the Grey Cup. The newspapers were full of this stuff about how when the chips are down and the dew is on the pumpkin, the big tough Hamiltons will rise up and kill you.

The game was played in Toronto. The crowd was 25,723. That tells you something, too, compared to subsequent years when any such game involving my Argos would be a sellout every time. And for a while it looked as if all the legends were true. I was very conscious of John Bassett, in the royal box up behind the bench, when we kicked off to start the game and Hamilton drove the ball down our throats in the next few plays and scored a touchdown. They kicked off, took the ball away from us and scored again. After only half a quarter, it was 14-0 and looked as if it could go to 50-0.

Hamilton got the ball a third time and walked down the field as if they owned it, before finally we held them and took over somewhere around our 10-yard line. And then we did it to them. Bill Symons tore off a 100-yard run and scored, with a great block by Jim Dillard shaking him loose. We marched down again and got a field goal. We got some big catches from Bobby Taylor and Neil Smith. They were still leading us 14-10 at the quarter, but by halftime we were ahead 27-21. We scored two field goals in the second half and manhandled them mercilessly to win it 33-21. That was the end of the Hamilton domination of Argos in playoffs during my years. We beat them in every playoff series we had.

I went to the dressing room. It was bedlam. They were yelling and shouting. Bobby Taylor might even have said something nice to Wally Gabler, it was that emotional – beating Hamilton and showing them what the new Argos stood for. In the middle of it all, coaches and players and reporters, John Bassett strode into the room with his coat open, hoarse from yelling, and put his arm around my shoulders and took me aside. He told me they were going to tear up my contract. He'd give me a new one for five years at more than $25,000 a year, with a new car and some kind of an expense account better than the one I had. As it turned out, I should have asked him to put it on paper right then and sign it.

That win put us into the Eastern final against Ottawa. I knew in my heart that we weren't that good, yet; not really good enough to beat Ottawa on personnel alone. On spirit, maybe. Russ Jackson then was at the peak of his power as Ottawa quarterback. If our defense was holding Ottawa's running game and holding its passing game, he'd start rolling out and running the ball himself. When we adjusted to contain him, he'd go back to passing or running. His skills were backed up by tremendous physical strength and high IQ. He was classic. Yet with this team I had, nothing was impossible.

In the first game of the two-game final, we beat them. It was only 13-11, giving us a two-point edge going into the second game. But as it turned out, when we went to Ottawa a week later, Wally Gabler came up awful flat. They led 22-0 at the half. Mike Blum was knocked silly with a concussion early. He tried to take out Moe Racine, the Ottawa offensive tackle. Racine jumped up and smashed his knee into Blum's helmet. Mike Wadsworth injured a knee badly. If we'd been able to hold them in the second half we might have come back but without Blum and Wadsworth we couldn't do it. The only bright part was that when Gabler couldn't get anything going, Tom Wilkinson went in and got us two touchdowns. The final score was 36-14 and Ottawa went on to win the Grey Cup against Calgary, while my coaches and I fanned out through the U.S. to scout college players for next year. But there were some satisfactions. Bill Symons had become the first Argonaut to rush for more than 1,000 yards, with 1,107, and the first Argonaut to win the C.F.L. Player of the Year Schenley award. And we placed eight men on the All-Star team.

If I'd been in danger of getting a swelled head over the amount of progress we'd made in two years, something that happened late January helped cure it. There was that little matter of a new contract that John Bassett had mentioned. When I went into sign it, Lew Hayman had something else in mind: four years instead of five and no new car. Lew told me frankly that he had changed Bassett's mind. I wondered how a guy like Bassett could make this kind of gesture and then back down. It made me see what a powerful position Lew had with Bassett.

Also, I could see the possibility of more trouble ahead. My conviction that Gabler was not the right man to get the most out of this football club now was so strong I wanted to do something about it. I didn't tell Wilkinson, or anybody else, but I was convinced that Wilkinson had to be given a chance.

I don't suppose there were ever two men in the same job less alike than Wilkinson and Gabler. Wilkinson was five feet ten. When he was with the Rifles, the other guys used to call him Groceries because of his paunch. He was from a small place in Wyoming and at that time always dressed in rumpled clothes off the field, with often as not a two-day beard. He chewed tobacco and spat the juice very accurately up to about six feet. Definitely not the Argonaut boardroom type and I knew that Bassett tended to dismiss him as just a refugee from the Continental league, one of my little foibles.

My line of thinking about Gabler and Wilkinson, all thoroughly discussed with my associate coaches, was developed weeks before our 1969 training camp opened. Edmonton called me in May and asked if I'd be interested in trading Al Irwin, a good pass-catching end. They knew that I had another excellent young Canadian, Paul Markle, as Irwin's backup, good enough to challenge for the first-string job. So we talked. I mentioned Ron Forwick, their young defensive end. When we were kicking names around, they came up with Frank Cosentino. All my antenna stood up straight. Cosentino was a real rarity, an experienced Canadian quarterback. He'd played well in Hamilton at the beginning of his career, an understudy for Bernie Faloney. He'd played well at Edmonton, in and out of the first-string job. He had great credentials to be a backup man who could go in, in any given game, and get the job done on his own. Most football clubs had to carry two U.S. quarterbacks (Russ Jackson in Ottawa was the exception as an All-Star Canadian at that position). If I could get Cosentino there would be a chain reaction throughout the football team. I'd be able to play a U.S. player at some other position that needed strengthening. Also, I'd have either Wilkinson or Gabler available to trade for another top-line player, if the chance came up. I made the trade for Cosentino.

I don't want to give the impression that my life with the Argonauts was one long problem in relations with top management, but there was a strike of players when training camp opened that June. They had asked in March for a change in the pay system during training camp. We gave imports $50 a week spending money but nothing to anybody else, except that all players were billetted at St. Andrew's College at Aurora for rooms and meals. This made it possible that a Canadian player could go through training camp and be dropped without being paid a cent. The system could have stood improvement but that was not directly my business. My business was to get the damn football team into camp and get ready for the season. I was very upset by the strike. People told me later I shouldn't have intervened and maybe they were right, but it's not my habit to stand back from something that affects me deeply. The day camp opened, only one player, Grant McKee, and the rookies showed up. Seventeen of last year's regulars didn't.

Around June 17, Lew Hayman assured me that management was adamant. They'd made some concessions and that was it. They wouldn't be blackmailed by a strike. The players, instead of reporting to Aurora, were keeping in shape by working out at Port Credit high school. On the definite word I'd had from Hayman, I laid my own relationship with the players on the line. I went to the school, we all got into a room and I told them, "Take my word as your coach, I'm not kidding, they are not going to make another concession. If you don't accept what they've offered you'll all be suspended, put out of football for this year and we'll have to find a new football team." When I was finished they asked me to leave the room. A little later they called me back. They appreciated me coming, they said, but were going to strike anyway.

Next day I'm called to a meeting at Bassett's office. Some of the other directors were there – Charles Dubin, the lawyer, who's now a Supreme Court judge; Len Lumbers, who later became my greatest enemy on the board of directors. Hayman was also there. The first thing they talked about was making more concessions.

I stood up. "Listen," I said. "I went out there on the basis that you told that this was as far as we were going to go. I gave the players my word that they weren't going to get anything else. If you go any further now they will never believe me again. They'll think I just went out there as part of your goddam power play. If you were going to relent you should have told me and I wouldn't have gone out at all. This way you make a liar out of me. I'm suggesting right now that we suspend them all and I get on the blower and start contacting players to replace them."

When I got done, Lumbers and the whole bunch of them said, "Leo's right. Okay. Let's suspend them." We called a press conference and announced that. It was headlines that day. Then the next day, June 19, more headlines. The newspapers said that Wally Gabler, as spokesman, made an eleventh-hour call to Bassett telling him that they'd come back and play for the concessions already made plus an agreement that at the end of the football season Bassett would negotiate with them further. The story made it like a personal intervention, Gabler to the rescue. But I heard from Bobby Taylor just in the spring of 1972 that he was in Gabler's apartment at the time – what the hell he'd be doing there I don't know – and that Bassett was the one who made the call and promised the year-end conference. One more concession. So he managed to make a fool out of me anyhow.

I was glad it was over, of course. But it gave me an insight into my relationship with the players. I'd been crazy enough to think that when I went out there as their father confessor, their friend, their confidant, their coach, that they would think enough of me to go along. Instead of, like jerks, refusing me but responding to Bassett, hat in hand.

It was just one of those things that I had to swallow. At camp I requested that they come in one at a time. The only thing I asked each one was, "Are you ready to play? And help us into the Grey Cup?" And the 100 per cent reply was, "Yes, I sure am, Coach." Very humbly. That was it. I forgot about it. Or almost, until now.

Funny thing, that season the last guy in town who thought Tom Wilkinson was going to be the Argonaut quarterback was Tom Wilkinson. In workouts Gabler had the first team, Cosentino the second, Wilkinson the third. It was like me at Illinois the year Ray Eliot kept me with the fourth team right up until I suddenly was a starter in the first game. Early in the camp Wilkinson told a newspaperman, "When I get cut I'm going to stop at Winnipeg, Calgary, and Vancouver on the way home." Not if I get cut – when I get cut. This wasn't lack of confidence in his own ability. He said, "I can play for any team in the West except Regina." Regina had perennial All-Star Ron Lancaster. He also said, "I can play for Argos, too, but there's no way. I'm here as insurance in case Wally Gabler gets hurt. Wally is going to be No. 1 here and Cosentino will be backup."

All I said in comment was, "He's competing for the job. He's gonna play."

I gave Wilkinson his chance in our exhibition games. He didn't change my mind at all about what he could do. After he steered us to a good win in Vancouver late in July, the B.C. coach, Jim Champion, said to me, "Looks like you got to go with Wilkinson." I said I at least had to keep giving him a chance.

At the beginning of the season, I kept right on. He started our first three games. We won them all and he was leading all C.F.L. passers with 34 completions out of 55 attempted, 806 yards gained by air, seven touchdown passes.

What made the performance even more satisfying to me was that about the first of August I saw a real chance that our unique position in having three good quarterbacks in camp might work to strengthen another part of the team.

Winnipeg was in trouble at quarterback and to get one was willing to give up a player I'd always wanted – Dave Raimey. I didn't have to be a genius to see that if we could take advantage of this situation we'd have the best pair of running backs in Canada. Bill Symons, of course, was the other one. I was having contract trouble with him because he'd only been making $14,000 a year when he won the Schenley award in 1968. He deserved a good raise but not what he was asking. He was talking about playing out his option. I thought we'd have had a better chance with him, a different atmosphere, if we'd done something I suggested the year before when he won the Schenley. I knew what he was being paid then, not a great deal because he hadn't made our football club until the last cut. He and his wife would have to go to a lot of football functions because of this award, costing money for new clothes, and so on. I suggested that the club give them $1,000 as a gesture for winning the Schenley, tell them to buy clothes or spend it as they wanted, and that we'd talk contract later. That might have put him in a different frame of mind at contract time. But the club didn't do it.

88

I thought he'd sign eventually. The idea of teaming him with Raimey, together with the way Wilkinson was going, made my mouth water. Ottawa wanted Raimey, too, but didn't have what Winnipeg needed, a quarterback, to trade.

I always thought Raimey was one of the best running backs of all time. Indescribable. He didn't run, he floated. He was like a ghost. He would seem to be just tippy-toeing, didn't look physically strong but he had great strength in his legs for breaking tackles. Ever since I'd come to Argos I'd been thinking that if we could just get Raimey on our football team. . . .

Raimey knew I admired him. I'd told him. And after four years in Winnipeg, he wanted to get out. He would call me privately five or six times a year asking if there was any way I could get him to Toronto. Now I had a chance – a quarterback to deal, with Winnipeg starved for a quarterback. In late July or early August I talked to the Winnipeg coach, Joe Zaleski. Joe was a difficult guy for me to negotiate with. Like a lot of other coaches he always felt that I was trying to pick his pockets. Still, I got out of him the possibility Raimey would be available. They were having problems. In Winnipeg, they called Raimey Peck's Bad Boy. Zaleski sent him home to Winnipeg after a blowup on a trip to Hamilton; an argument Raimey had with their quarterback of the time, John Schneider. Raimey, in this and other ways, was getting a reputation of being unmanageable. That probably meant he would fit in very nicely with our group.

If Zaleski suspected me of being devious, he was right to this extent: he thought that the quarterback I really didn't want to lose was Gabler, because he'd been our first stringer for three seasons. So he said he'd take Gabler for Raimey; a star for a star, not knowing that I'd already decided Gabler was expendable.

Still, that was only my own idea, so far. When I first talked to Zaleski, knowing the way I was leaning about Gabler, I went to Hayman about it. I got the message loud and clear that the Argonaut management would be strongly against trading Gabler. I had to consider that and I did. It only made me more and more sold on the idea. I could have knuckled under. Zaleski would have taken Wilkinson instead – he had to have somebody. Eventually I decided that, since I believed in this, I would have to fight for it, even knowing the place Gabler had in the affections of John Bassett.

Around the middle of August, I was very close to that decision. Winnipeg was in Toronto for a game with us and a funny thing happened that night. Raimey was making one of those toe-dance end runs toward our bench. Marvin Luster was always put in charge of Raimey whenever we played Winnipeg. Marvin's job was to go with Raimey wherever he went and to mishandle him as much as possible. Luster dumped Raimey right in my lap on the sidelines, very hard. As Raimey got up he looked at me, and on an impulse I said, "Hey, save yourself! You're coming with me!"

He took a couple of steps back towards the huddle and then stopped and said, "You mean it?"

This was right in the middle of our game. To tell the truth, I said it mostly to influence him, get him thinking so that maybe his concentration would be disturbed and he wouldn't play too hard against us.

But a day or two later I had to act. I went in to see Lew Hayman. He was still absolutely against the deal. It had been enlarged a little by then. We were also going to get Chip Barrett thrown in. He'd been a regular with Winnipeg the year before as a defensive halfback, a Canadian. (We'd sent him to Winnipeg in the first place, as part of the deal for Dick Thornton.) I argued, reminding Lew that part of our arrangement was that I was in complete charge of player changes. Finally he told me that he was against the deal personally and knew Bassett would be. I knew that too. In one brief discussion I'd had with him on the subject, he'd been rather threatening. But, Lew said if that was the way I wanted to do it, it was my baby.

I asked him the question that was on the top of my mind. "If I make the deal, knowing the way John Bassett feels about Gabler, can I be fired for it?"

He said something like, "If they fire you, they'll have to fire me, too, because I'm the one who put you in charge. Even though I do disagree, I'll stand behind you."

John Bassett was in Nova Scotia at Herb Solway's summer place there. I got the number and phoned him. I wasn't phoning to ask if I could make the deal but I owed him the courtesy of seeing that he heard about it firsthand, from me. I told him that I had made up my mind to trade Gabler and keep Wilkinson.

At that time, on things I suggested that he didn't approve, he might make objections but he wouldn't say, No, you can't do that. Later he did order me to do or not do things but we'll come to that. He didn't order me not to trade Gabler. He just implied very strongly that if I did it, I'd better be prepared to win, I'd better be right. "Well, if that's the way you think you should go . . . " he said and didn't end the sentence or say goodbye. Click, went the phone.

That, I guess, was the beginning of a long under the surface (for a while) struggle I had with Bassett and the other directors. Mainly because I had put my money on, to them, the wrong quarterback.

A few hours later we announced the Gabler for Raimey deal. If anything had been needed to feed football fever in Toronto, getting Raimey was it, plus Wilkinson's shambling style and color. We'd had only two sellouts in 1968. In 1969 we had seven. When Raimey flew in we rolled out the red carpet for him all the way from the airport to the practice field. I assigned Bob Gibson to work with him night and day to study the playbook and get him into the game we had coming up with Vancouver. Early in September the very strong Regina team came in, heading for a 13-3 season and the Western championship, and we manhandled them 34-15. Later that month we beat Montreal 36-33 in what some players said was the dirtiest game they'd ever played in; the one where Sonny Wade stepped on Jim Tomlin's head after a tackle and called Ed Harrington a black nigger. He apologized to Tomlin but not to Harrington. The football commissioner, Jake Gaudaur, just sort of pooh-

poohed the idea that there should be a fine on either count. We beat Hamilton 17-7 on October 13 and six days later, in Toronto, hammered them again with the crowd chanting in the late stages, "We want fifty!" We gave it to them, 51-8. I heard later that Ralph Sazio, the Hamilton general manager, said after that game that he'd get even with me if it was the last thing he did. And he did try, in later years.

We beat Montreal again in November in a very rough game, paying off Sonny Wade – although to hand it to him, he didn't intimidate. The only team we couldn't beat in that stretch, before we finished the season with 10 wins and four losses, was Ottawa. Raimey had torn some knee ligaments in the Hamilton game and was gone for the season. That weakened us. Ottawa beat us 20-9 to clinch first place with 11 wins to our 10. It was the best Toronto win record since 1960 and our 406 scoring points was the best in the club's history. Not bad production for a quarterback our brass didn't want.

Again we knocked off Hamilton in the semi-final and again faced the final against Ottawa. Even though Wilkinson had been bothered late in the season with a shoulder injury, he challenged Ottawa hard in the first game. We beat them 22-14. At the end Wilkinson rushed over to shake hands with Jackson. I called him back. I didn't go for that fraternity bullshit, falling into the trap where the next time you meet him you aren't razor sharp because it's difficult to hate somebody when you know that at the end of the game you're going to be shaking hands.

And then a few days later in the Playback Club meeting looking ahead to the second half of the final, I made a statement that later made me want to cut my tongue out. "It will take an act of God to beat us on Saturday," I said. From coast to coast, it was one of those quotable quotes that you always wish you didn't say. What I meant was we knew physically we were getting close enough to Ottawa to win and that unless somebody breaks a leg, or unless the weather is terrible, or there's a bad-break fumble or something, we're going to win. But that isn't how it sounded in the papers, especially in Ottawa. It was just what they needed to get psyched up for the second game. And if that wasn't enough, that was Russ Jackson Day, because he was retiring and if we won it would be his last game of football. I thought it was unbelievable for the league to allow that before such an important game. It could happen nowhere else but in the Canadian Football League, wherever the name professional is applied. In a game so important, to give the home team the advantage of having a day for their all-time great player, to psyche them up, I thought was pure bush. Somehow the commissioner never bothered to assert himself on that issue.

The act of God the Ottawa fans said they'd produce – having Russ Jackson walk across the Rideau Canal without getting his feet wet – didn't happen. But another did – a badly frozen, rutted field. The Ottawa players wore broomball shoes and I looked like a clown because we hadn't expected those conditions and it was too late for us to order special footgear. Maybe they would have beaten us anyway. Ronnie Stewart was running like a wild man that day and we were slipping and sliding and falling. Harrington was hurt early, out for the game. We looked terrible. Nothing Wilkinson or Cosentino did helped. They beat us 32-3.

The only consolation was that Ottawa went on and clobbered Saskatchewan almost as badly in the Grey Cup. But our performance in that last game didn't help me any with the people like Bassett who were still smarting over me keeping Wilkinson and trading Gabler. As a matter of fact, it told me something, too: that we still weren't set at quarterback, even if Wilkinson was a hell of an improvement over Gabler at that time.

Bassett
versus Corrigall: Beautiful

The toughest so-and-so I ever recruited in my life, and I have to laugh when I think back on parts of this, was Jim Corrigall in the spring of 1970. The first time I met him, Blackie was with me. We went down to Kent State University in Ohio and asked the way to Corrigall's room. He had one on the basement floor of the dormitory. I knocked on his door and he said, "Come on in."

I opened the door. It was in the middle of winter. The windows were wide open. He was lying on a bed with no sheets, no pillowcase, no blankets or anything else. Just with a pair of big boots on, khaki pants and a jacket. Six feet three, 245 pounds, 23 years old, captain of the Kent State team. He'd won about every award there was in the mid-American conference, had been chosen All-American by the Newspaper Enterprise Association, a team which is picked by pro scouts. On top of that he'd been a second draft choice of the St. Louis Cardinals, the highest a Canadian has ever been picked in the N.F.L. draft. And he was just lying there surveying. Lord of all he surveyed.

I said, "Jim, I'm Coach Cahill."

He looked at me as if I was nothing. "Yeah, Coach," he said. "Nice to see you."

I said, "I want to talk to you about. . . . "

"Yeah, Coach, I know, Coach. You want to talk to me about Toronto."

I said, "Let me ask you this, Jim. Do you have an open mind about where you'll play?"

"I'll play any place. I'll play where I get the best opportunity."

He was born in Barrie and went to school at Scollard Hall in North Bay before he got a scholarship at Kent State. But with any real good pro prospects, the nationalism thing, Canada first, isn't worth five cents as far as giving you an edge in signing. So I wasn't planning to mention that for a while. As it turned out, he did.

I said, "I think we have the right approach to things. I think that. . . ."

"Don't tell me about I'm a Canadian, now," he said, "I'm drafted by the St. Louis Cardinals and I can play down there. I love Canada and I'd prefer to live in Canada but I'm going to go where I get the best deal. What have you got in mind?"

Boy, we had the damnedest session you ever saw. I finally told him, "I don't know what keeps me from hitting you right in the head."

He said, "I think it is probably better judgement."

After we left, walking away, Blackie said, "I've never met anybody like that guy in my life." He was so hard to talk to, so suspicious of everything.

We kept after him in later visits. He knew all about Toronto. That's not necessarily an advantage for a kid from Barrie. For all towns and cities near Toronto, there's that Hogtown thing. Weeks went by. St. Louis was recruiting him, too. They offered him a hell of a contract. He was being advised by an uncle, Harry Savage of Orlando, who used to have a public relations business in Toronto. Savage knew the ropes, too, and in an affable way was just as tough as the kid. So was Jim's father, a rugged Irishman from Barrie. All of them wanted to see that Corrigall got the best deal coming.

It was all hanging in the balance, when John Bassett decided to apply the clincher. He's like that. Sometimes he's good at it, waiting until a deal is almost set up and then making the final push in person with money, promises or concessions, decisions that he could make on the spur of the moment, without consulting anybody else.

We had pretty well prepared what we were going to pay the kid. The visit to Bassett was going to be the end-all; the chairman of the board special. So we went up to the marble tower, Bassett's office in the *Telegram*. It was a cherished experience.

Bassett got up and proceeded to stride back and forth with his thumbs in his belt. All the time, he was talking. "Now, Mr. Corrigall," he began. "This is what we have to offer *you*." In his special way, you know. Forceful. Splendid. This big kid from Barrie was sitting on a chair. "I'm not going to have you say anything," Bassett told him. "You just listen to what I have to say." He stopped at the Bobby Kennedy picture from time to time. He talked for a half hour. I could tell he thought he was just overwhelming the guy. At the end he said, "Now, Mr. Corrigall, what do you have to say?"

Corrigall stretched out his legs with those size 13s so that his neck was just about resting on the back of the chair, his heels on the floor, and said, "Well, Mr. Bassett, I'm not too impressed."

The look Bassett gave! He didn't know whether to go to the bathroom or wind his watch.

Corrigall said, "I want you to know what I want. Well, I'd like this . . . and I want that . . . and I'd like to have this . . . and I want this . . . and I want that . . . and I want this . . . . " Each one was either money, pension, fringe benefit, you name it.

"And maybe if everything goes well and I make up my mind that way, maybe I'll come to Toronto," he said.

It was beautiful. I'm sure Bassett thought, well here he is and here is Bassett, chairman of the board, and I'm up here in this big office of mine and he's here and we're going to overpower him. But Corrigall was completely and totally uninterested in being overpowered.

Corrigall then just got up and went back home. I heard later from one of his teachers at Scollard Hall, Father Mike, a close confidant of Corrigall's, he'd pretty well decided to go to St.

Louis. A few days later (again from what I heard) Corrigall actually was on his way to St. Louis to sign. But on the way through Toronto he came in to listen to our final offer. We had jacked it up to a two-year contract at more money than ever had been offered to a Canadian player, plus a few bonuses and extras. But he wanted one more thing, something in the way of a pension bigger than the C.F.L. one. "Mr. Bassett," he said, "what can you do for me on that?"

What we did was work together a deal where at age 42 he gets a substantial cash settlement. That was to make up for the C.F.L. pension versus the N.F.L. Annually, it isn't really as much as it sounds, but it does commit the club to pay a few thousand a year over a 20-year period, to build a large lump sum. That's the deal that he got and when the contract was worked out and rewritten a few times, he signed it.

All through this, I took care to keep a close association with him, keep his confidence in me. He was as tough as he had to be on money but above and beyond everything else Corrigall needs to know that he can get along with the guy he is going to work for.

Apart from training camp and the season itself, recruiting is a pretty well constant pursuit. We kept tab on some players right through years of college. Blackie Johnston, Gord Ackerman, Jim Rountree, Bob Gibson, and I were all involved. The associate coaches would make the rounds of college spring training camps, introduce themselves to players we thought we might want. After our season, when many of big college games came up, we'd be there. We wouldn't be a nuisance or interfere with what a college coach was trying to do. That would have hurt us in the long run. It was often just a matter of shaking hands with a kid, telling him who we were and that we were interested. We fanned out to cover the bowl games the same way. Every pro club in North America does the same, of course. When we got a kid interested, we'd fly him into Toronto and show him the city, take him to the best restaurants, have him meet the other U.S. players and go out with them so they could talk things over. If a kid met a girl he liked along the way, of course, so much the better but the average pro club doesn't recruit with girls, no matter what you might hear. There are also a lot of stories about how Argos would go out flourishing big bankrolls. Well, money is important to any player or he wouldn't consider being a pro. My overall philosophy in recruiting was not so much in competing with other Canadian football teams but with the National Football League. If we could get a player for a little bit more than he was offered in the National Football League, we did a hell of a job. Most of U.S. kids basically want to play before their home audience, stay in the States, share the glamor of the big team names that were being covered in their hometown sports pages every day – which the C.F.L. is not, except for an occasional score. I think a lot of people have the misconception that Joe Theismann, Greg Barton, Jim Stillwagon, Leon McQuay, Eric Allen, Tim Anderson, Gene Mack, and others came to Canada because they got much more money than they could get in the N.F.L. That isn't necessarily so. With a lot of those guys we recruited pretty tight with what they would have been paid in the N.F.L.

It usually happens, incidentally, that in recruiting there is someone in the background. With Corrigall it was Harry Savage, his uncle. With some kids it is a paid agent or lawyer. The key is to find out who the kid listens to and make sure that he, the other guy, is taken into everyone's confidence all along the way.

In Tony Moro's case, also in 1970, this caused us trouble. Like Corrigall, Moro is a Canadian, although born in Italy. At De La Salle school in Toronto he played under a couple of former Argonauts and was a friend of Nobby Wirkowski. But also there was a dentist in Minnesota named Morgan, a boyhood friend of Tony's from Toronto, who had a lot of influence. When Tony wound up a good career at the University of Dayton and was picked as a 14th-round draft choice by the Washington Redskins, Dr. Morgan was torn between seeing him come to Canada, where he'd be making his life, or going to Washington to make it under Vince Lombardi. The Lombardi name was magic in recruiting. Also, from what Tony had heard about salaries for Canadians in the C.F.L., he certainly wanted to listen to the Washington offer.

I made several trips to Dayton to talk to Moro. He had a lot of natural ability, had played wide receiver, blocking back and fullback, and his coaches liked his temperament. These are the things that you are looking for. I made a visit down there in his junior year and took him out to dinner to get acquainted and tell him we were interested in him. In the end, it came down to money. Washington made a strong pitch. But we came up with a little better deal and when we sat down for our final discussion, Nobby Wirkowski made the difference. Tony trusted Nobby, who'd arranged to send him to college in the U.S. in the first place. Nobby said, "All b.s. aside, Tony, you're a Toronto boy and this is where you should be playing. You're getting a good contract offer from Leo here and personally I think this is where you should go." Nobby was the deciding factor. Tony played well for Argos, and maybe still hasn't reached his full potential.

Heavy recruiting doesn't always have a happy ending. Right at the time we were dealing with Tony, and later with Jim Corrigall, we were having to get rid of a guy we'd been very high on the year before, Vernon Vanoy. New York Giants had drafted him high and we'd signed him with a great fanfare but he hadn't worked out. We put him on waivers and Vancouver picked him up. We said he was traded for future considerations. That covers a multitude of sins. In this case it covered our tracks with the public we'd sold so big on Vanoy the year before.

We had one other major recruiting necessity in that spring of 1970. In February Frank Cosentino quit pro football. He'd promised me to play one more year because I wanted another go at the Wilkinson-Cosentino combination that had won 10 games for us the year before. But when he got a coaching offer from the University of Western Ontario, where he'd graduated in 1960, I couldn't stand in his way. It fitted him perfectly. He was completing his doctorate in physical education at the University of Alberta and this was the kind of job he might have for life, if he wanted it. Nothing in pro football would be for life.

That meant we needed another quarterback. I had exactly the one in mind – Don Jonas from Orlando in the Continental League. I'd been trying to get him since I signed with Argos myself. Away back in 1967 I'd brought him and his wife to Toronto to look around. In the research departments of a lot of pro football teams, he was rated as the best quarterback not playing in the N.F.L. or the A.F.L. But he had such a good deal in Orlando that nobody had been able to pry him loose – well-paid quarterback, sports director of a TV station, P.R. director for Royal Crown Cola. He'd played one game as a running back with the Philadelphia Eagles after he graduated from Penn State, then went to Newark in the Continental League. When that franchise was transferred to Orlando he went along and that's when he was developed by Perry Moss as a quarterback. He held all the league records for quarterbacks; also kicked field goals, his longest 52 yards, and had gone through two seasons without missing a convert in 56 attempts. A real prize prospect, even at 29. When I was in the Continental League, he always looked like a winner to me.

I called him one evening.

"Look," I said, "you tried with the Philadelphia Eagles as a running back and you were one of the last cuts. You're the kind of individual who'll spend all your lifetime wondering if you could have made it in professional football at a higher level. I think you owe it to yourself to come up here and prove to everybody what a good quarterback you are."

He listened. Then I went down there. I took the family for a break on the beaches. My wife reminds me quite often that when we stopped in Lexington, Kentucky, we didn't see any horses. Most of the time I was on the phone talking to Jonas.

When we finally did get to Florida and were on the beach, I didn't do much swimming, sunning, or playing with my kids. I was too preoccupied with how I was going to handle Jonas when I got to Orlando a couple of days later. Then I spent two or three days over in Orlando, taken out of my family's vacation. The earlier trip he'd taken to Toronto helped. He signed.

Once again we were in what I figured was a rare position in Canadian football – we had two topline quarterbacks, the best we'd ever had. The only thing I couldn't foresee was that John Bassett wasn't going to like Jonas, either.

Spare Me Those Cadillac Limousines

If I ever go to a psychiatrist I think he might be somewhat startled at two things that are traumatic experiences with me. One is when I hear the National Anthem. I'm in a movie and the lights go on and maybe I'm feeling great from laughing or whatever and then they play the anthem. Suddenly I'm tensed up tight enough to strum like a banjo. The second thing is the sight of a Cadillac limousine with chauffeur. I've figured both out for myself. The anthem thing is because usually when I hear the anthem it is at the start of a football game, with my mind racing over the dozens of hours we've spent getting ready to this point and wondering if it's all going to work. And I never see a big Cadillac and uniformed driver without thinking of times when the Argonaut directors wanted to see me. It was always trouble. There was no friendly phone call, saying, "Hey, Leo, we've got a few things we want to talk over with you. What time would it be convenient to you to meet us?" It was usually a call from John Bassett's male secretary, very formal: "The directors wish to see you at such and such a time. Mr. Bassett's driver will pick you up outside the stadium."

That's how it was on Tuesday, September 29, 1970. I can't say I wasn't expecting it after the way we'd played in Calgary two days before. Trouble had been building, from our first game of the season – when Sam Etcheverry and I renewed our old lack of rapport with one another. The Montreal club had been sold to Sam Berger of Ottawa the previous December. He'd installed Etcheverry as coach, Red O'Quinn as general manager, and J.I. Albrecht as O'Quinn's assistant and director of playing personnel. They beat us in their opening game at home by one touchdown, 34-27. Then we beat Edmonton and Hamilton. But late in August in Winnipeg we'd been waylaid 28-22 by Wally Gabler, playing one of his occasional flawless games at quarterback, plus Bill Frank – whom we'd let go on a contract dispute – getting the Winnipeg lines high as kites against us. I knew one repercussion of that one, that Bassett stormed out to the *Telegram*'s sports department complaining that football writer Al Sokol had been far too easy on us and wanting his (ahem) quite fair and objective story killed; which he was talked out of. Dick Thornton and Bobby Taylor both were hurt, Thornton for 30 days and Taylor for most of the season. Playing short these regulars we lost in Regina a few days later 36-14, even worse than in Winnipeg.

Then came a fairly famous pair of games with Ottawa. We went in there on Labour Day with two wins and three losses and getting some blasts all around. Sniping. *This is the team that's supposed to win the Grey Cup this year?* That kind of stuff. The players were getting worked up. The word was out that our directors were not impressed at all with either of our quarterbacks. Anyway, we went to Ottawa fired up to get moving. On the first Ottawa offensive play of the game their new (in 1970) quarterback, Gary Wood, ran a pitchout to his right and Ed Harrington came in on his blind side. Wood was charitable enough to say later he was sure Harrington thought he still had the ball. Coach Jack Gotta said he didn't come in late, it was just a hammer job. He was picking up Frank Clair's vocabulary. But anyway Harrington hit Wood with his forearm and looked as if he'd torn his head off. Harrington was ejected from the game for unnecessary roughness, then and there. But that didn't slow us down. Jonas went all the way until the last three minutes and completed 17 passes out of 32. Bill Symons scored four touchdowns and everything was roses until the Thursday of that week, when C.F.L. Commissioner Jake Gaudaur suspended Harrington for one game and fined him $200.

I was infuriated. So was Lew Hayman. In the same game, Billy Joe Booth had drilled Raimey after the whistle, when he was on the ground, out of bounds. No penalty. Why pick on us to start suspending players for roughness?

The thing that really galled me was that we not only lost Harrington for the entire Ottawa game but because of the suspension lost him for the next game, too, also with Ottawa. And if they were going to set a precedent on throwing people out of the Canadian Football League it reminded me that Commissioner Jake Gaudaur was the same man, wearing a different hat as Hamilton's president, when Angelo Mosca stiffed Willie Fleming on the sidelines in the Grey Cup in 1963. Jake went out on the field after that game and raised Mosca's hand above his head in triumph. It was very difficult for me to understand that now because he was in a different office it suddenly wasn't just tough football to do a thing like that, but a crime.

The thing we felt worst about was the reflection on Harrington, one of the finest persons I've ever coached. All of his coaches since he was in the eighth grade taught him the football philosophy that when you hit the football field, you change personalities. It is hit or be hit. When they suspended him he was working for a boys' home in Toronto, looked upon by everyone as a gentleman. All of a sudden he's labelled a criminal. Ottawa called him a killer.

Nobody can equate the effect of a Booth or Harrington on their football team. They keep everybody honest. They take the edge away from the quarterbacks doing fancy things because the quarterbacks spend most of their time looking over their shoulders. I knew that when Ottawa came to Toronto with Harrington off the football team, they wouldn't have to be looking for him. It would give them a little added confidence. In that game Harrington was up in the stands. He wasn't allowed in the dressing room. So before the game I talked to some players about this game and how Ottawa was going to try to make up with cheap shots and everything else for what Harrington was accused of doing. I told them, Keep your heads up and make damn sure you don't lock your cleats in the ground after the play and get blindsided and get put out for the season. Let's win today for a guy who has made a great contribution to this team. We all know what kind of a guy he is. Let's win and then we'll present him with the game ball to show everybody what we think of him.

We won, 30-25. Then there was a sight that anyone who was there or watched it on TV remembers. It was dripping rain. Usually, the game ball presentation is made in private, in the dressing room, to the guy the players think contributed the most. But this time our whole team stayed out on the field, looking for Harrington. We put a call on the loudspeaker for him and finally he came down. I think it was Danny Nykoluk, the captain, who gave him the ball but I was standing right there and I sensed that Harrington knew I was behind it. A lot of people interpreted this as a grandstand thing by me to slap the commissioner in the face. But it really was more. Harrington had been such a model guy and such a coachable guy and such a good person. I thought this would help erase the public indictment against him in front of all those kids that he worked with day in and day out.

What I was thinking was, Ed, we started together and you've done a lot for me and I hope I've done something for you. He had tears in his eyes and knew what I was trying to do. I didn't give a shit about what the commissioner or anyone else would say.

Frank Clair later on was to say in his own slow-talking way, "Well, Cahill, he's a good coach and he's done a good job over there . . . but that Harrington thing, that was bad." He held that in his craw forever. Everytime he'd talk about me he'd say something nice but then, "Cahill, ooh, that Harrington thing, that was bad."

Gaudaur shrugged it off. He said he'd left the park before it happened. "But there are more important football matters to be concerned about. I take no offense, if any was intended."

That game made us four wins and three losses before Montreal beat us again, 24-17, in Toronto. The press and public got on us about one play in the game. We were behind 16-10 in the fourth quarter when I sent in a play hoping for a cheap touchdown. There is always a justification for one of these plays in certain circumstances and this was one of them. Montreal had played exceptionally well defensively with two or three deep interceptions on Jonas and we weren't moving the football. It was a close enough game that we could break their back with one trick play and if so it would demoralize them because they had played so well defensively all day. So I told Dave Mann to throw a pass off a third down punt situation at our 40-yard line. There was no way they'd be expecting a pass. It was supposed to be thrown to Moro over his inside shoulder, away from the safety. Dave threw it on the outside shoulder toward the coverage and Al Phaneuf was alert enough to intercept. From there they went down and scored their winning touchdown.

It's the kind of play about which, if it works, everybody says, "Ah, that Cahill, hasn't he got a lot of imagination?" If it doesn't work it brings on one of the great football cliches of all time, that it's a high school play – even though trick plays score touchdowns every year, sometimes are seen in the N.F.L., and even have been used in the Super Bowl, if a coach thinks the time is ripe. Every team has them. We can't all be high school coaches. It just seems that way in the press box when one doesn't work.

So our record was a very modest four wins and four losses when we got ready to go to Calgary for the September 27 game.

We had good workouts all week. You can get a feeling from a team in practice and the feeling this time was good. We thought that if we could win this one on the road we'd be in pretty good shape for a playoff position. So we get on the plane and suddenly we were engulfed in a real carnival atmosphere. Football fans everywhere. Herb Kearney, a good friend of mine, was one of the founders of the Argonaut Playback Club and was my gin partner on the trip. Herb was one of those who helped the Argos. The coaches drove cars from Hearn Pontiac, Herb's dealership.

I said to Herb, "Where in the world did all these people come from?"

"This is the Playback Club group," he said.

I'd known they were coming to the game but not that they were going to be on the same plane with us. All the way out there we had those fans, all eager to look at the players and get close to them and talk to them a bit, a complete distraction from our normal procedure, just not a healthy pre-game atmosphere.

We got to the hotel in Calgary and I can see this circus atmosphere continuing, this mardi gras thing, with the coaches and the fans and the players and let's have a party type of thing. It just teed me off. I knew what an important game it was.

I probably handled the problem in a very crude way. But there are certain times in football when I feel, especially when getting ready for an important game, that it's a good time to have a crisis. Sometimes I'd create a crisis. Maybe jump on the guy they like the most on the football team. Then they'd say, "What the hell is he doing, getting on Symons?" or whatever. And this would rattle them a little bit, shake them up. Then they would go out and work harder because they were mad. I didn't think it out this time but I knew I had to do something. I strolled over to the desk. The players are all around, asking for messages from aunts and uncles and girl friends and everything else. More carnival. It just made me mad, added to the frustration of having all those fans on the plane and now here in the lobby too.

I walked up to the desk and told the man, "Give me the messages." Then I turned around. All these guys are waiting for their messages. I said, "If anyone wants to see you they can come down here and see me and in turn I'll have them come down and talk to you. As far as the phone calls and those things are concerned, forget it. No calls in the rooms. And I'm going to keep these messages."

I didn't think about it much more at the time. There was a time earlier in Montreal when we were there for a key game before the playoffs and I said no phones hooked up in the rooms, no going to movies, no nothing. Stay in your room, except for our meetings. I can remember Dave Mann and a couple of them being highly indignant that they were being treated like kids. But that time we went out and won, did what we had to do. In Calgary it was my best judgement at the time to shake them up and get them thinking about the football game. But some players on our team really took this as a personal affront.

Whether this had anything to do with the way they played the next day, I don't know. But they were just awful. Calgary was almost as bad, at first. Playing our normal game we would have beaten them easily. But they came out of it and we didn't. They were leading us 27-0 late in the fourth quarter before we finally got a couple of touchdowns. And I guess all the directors were watching it on television. I didn't blast the players. I just told them that if they'd been worried about criticism before now they were going to get it more than ever and it would be justified.

I could tell what was likely to happen by the way some of the football writers acted. I usually get along with the press. But here we'd been, four and four going into this game, now four and five. Still five games to go. Not hopeless by any means. And we'd had injuries in August to a couple of important guys, Bobby Taylor and Dick Thornton. Taylor was still out. Still, these reporters sought out Lew Hayman after the game and asked, "What's going to happen, Lew? What are you going to do about it?" As if to say, "Look, this is the end of the world. Fire the son-of-a-bitch and hire someone else."

Lew was very disgusted, as I was, but I show it. Lew shows no emotion before a game, after a game or anything in between. He looks just as sad after a big win as after a big loss. A complete ice man. But they were all riding him and he was very upset. The game must have looked worse to him in the stands than it looked to me from the sidelines and I was ready to vomit. And there was this pressure on him from the press: what were they going to do? When were they going to make a move?

So we came back to Toronto. Then on Monday I get the big call: "The limousine is on the way. Get ready and come to the Granite Club."

My first reaction, I swear to God, in every one of these circumstances was never one of fear, never one of, "Oh, my God, are they going to fire me?" It was always one of complete resentment. Completely being turned off. How could these son-of-a-bitches question me when these are the circumstances, these are the facts, and we're going to play ourselves out of this but give us a chance. What the hell good is it to take me out of my office for four hours on the day I'm trying to get started on preparing for the next game? All the reporters knew at the time was that I wasn't around. They might have suspected why. My coaches knew why. But they said I was out to lunch. Some lunch.

I get to the Granite Club. Big pillars. High ceilings. Pure aristocratic Toronto. The directors were sitting around under a big chandelier in a room big enough to play a basketball game in.

I guess I should introduce them. Bassett you know, chairman of the board. Hayman you know, president and chief executive officer. Joe Wright, vice-chairman, I'd always liked. He was an old football player and oarsman, usually in the background and didn't have that much control over the situation anyway. Bill Ross, a beautiful person, used to come down to the practice every Thursday and lunch with the coaches and talk to the players. But not one of the power men. Charles Burns, Sr., was a very sophisticated man. Gave everyone the benefit of the doubt but in the long run he would probably go with the majority on will Leo go or will he stay? He wouldn't assert himself to hurt me any more than he would go out of his way to help me.

Another director was Charles Dubin, the lawyer for the

team, who subsequently went to the Supreme Court. He knew very little about football. He was always making remarks about how a game should be played and what we should do. He is a very clever lawyer and was fair or even kind to me in other ways but I never heard him say anything much about football that sounded as though it made sense.

That brings us to Len Lumbers, Sr. Lew Hayman later told me that Lumbers' dislike for me transcended anything he'd ever seen in a coach-director relationship. At one time he was quite cordial to me, always glad-handing everybody and calling the assistant coaches by the wrong names. And telling me about flying down to the Caribbean or some place to have lunch with the president of General Electric or something. Talking to hear himself talk. Then all of a sudden he just turned against me.

Anyway, the directors – I can't be sure they all were there – were sitting around waiting when I came in. It reminded me a little of one of those 007 movies. You know, they were just about ready to commission me to go out and stop the atomic bomb or something. Then they started. Lumbers and Bassett I can remember very vividly. They told me, in a sort of duet, that I had to make an example to this football team. It was going down hill. They said, we think the best example we can make is to fire those two quarterbacks and pick a couple of other key personnel and get rid of them. We'll start all over again if we have to. . . . We'll just start completely all over again.

I listened to about as much of this shit as I could. Then I pushed my chair back and said, "Well, evidently you want to run the football team. And you want to make the decisions on the football team. If you do, fire me. But if I'm going to run the football team, I'll tell you what we are going to do – we're not going to make any changes at all. Because that's not my style and that's not what I've done in the past and we're not going to panic." When I got warmed up I was going pretty good. In the end – and this took some time – they said in effect, "Well, it's your team. Handle it the way you want to. But you better do something."

I went back to the football team and got them into the meeting room where we usually show game films. Rather than stand up and talk to them I took a chair, put it against the desk and sat on the desk with my feet up on the chair. I told them exactly what had transpired. I can still remember Jonas sitting in the front, spellbound, with a cigar in his mouth listening to me. And Wilkinson. The two they'd wanted me to fire.

"This is what they wanted to do," I said. "They wanted to fire you and start all over again. But you're my people and I've got confidence in you. We've overcome these things before and we've got to get together and do it again. Now that you know what we're faced with, put up or shut up. You know I'm going to stick with you. If we go down, we're going to go down together." Melodramatic, no doubt. But that was a hell of a melodramatic day. No kidding.

I must say that this produced a certain extra earnestness about our preparations for the next five games. But because you can only play them one at a time (as coaches are always supposed to say), the first concentration was on Hamilton for the following Sunday. We'd beaten them 29-3 in August. That made our last two league scores against them total something like 80-11. They'd be laying for us. So we settled down to work on doing something a little bit different to throw them off. We knew pretty well how they were going to prepare for us. They would work out defenses to take away our outside running with Raimey and Symons. They also would take away our sprint pass with Wilkinson and some of the other things that we did best. But the last thing in the world that they would ever expect is that we would let Wilkinson run with the football. He wasn't physically that kind of a guy. He could scramble enough when he had to, but as a regular runner he couldn't do it. So we put in an option series which concentrated on sending him into the short side away from strength of the formation. Our tendencies throughout the year, which they knew from our films, had been to go to formation and go to strength. So we worked on this short side option series all week.

There was one little off-the-field sidelight. Herb Solway, my friend as well as Bassett's friend, called me for dinner a day or two after the Granite Club fiasco. He was interested in how I'd taken the showdown with the directors. I told him I could understand some people panicking but I'd been disappointed that John Bassett had allied himself with them instead of seeing the matter in its larger perspective. Frankly, I was hoping those sentiments would get back to Bassett. It was an uneasy week preparing for Hamilton with the Granite Club pressure still ringing in my mind. I kept remembering my hotheaded invitation for them to fire me. I didn't really want that. But on the night before the Hamilton game Bassett phoned me at my home. "Co-o-o-ach," he said, drawing it out, and went on in a friendly way, giving me reassurance. He was often like that, backing me up when I most needed it. When things got really rough, he came through.

So I felt a lot better about everything when we went to Hamilton the next morning, toting our little surprise, the short option series. The first couple of times that Wilkinson ran it he cut into gaping holes. And Hamilton got so upset to think that Wilkinson was beating them running with the football that it screwed them up as far as their game plan was concerned.

For us, at the start, it was just window-dressing. In my preparation for a game I've always been firmly convinced that you should do something they're not expecting. You're prepared later to go with fundamental stuff which has been working for you and occasionally you put in one of those crazy plays when you try to score in a hurry. The surprise stuff is useful at the start. You know the other team has prepared for you just like you prepared for them. In practice we defend all week long what they have been doing best over a five-game period of time. The coaches break down what the opposition usually does on each yard line, what is their tendency on the hash marks, what is their tendency in the middle of the field, what is their tendency on first and second down. Breaking all this stuff down you get a format to follow, a tendency sheet that we refer to when we really need something.

So starting every football game with something completely different than we'd used before gives them something to look at. They say, "Well, shit, this isn't what we've been working on all week." We might not have great success with it but sometimes we'd score with it simply because they weren't used to it. It would confuse them. Then when we'd go back to the stuff that we'd been using all season, they'd still be looking for the new stuff, our window-dressing.

When we started that day with Wilkinson on the option stuff we didn't have any visions that we were going to go a whole football game with Wilkinson running like hell. But it threw them off so completely we stayed with it. As a result we had won the football game before he was hurt in the third quarter and Jonas came in. The final score was 33-14 and it was a hell of a morale boost after what we'd been through at Calgary. To say nothing of the Granite Club.

This is probably the time to explain the Jonas-Wilkinson situation. Over the whole season, this was a controversial matter with the press and the fans, who tended to choose up sides between the two. In most games I used them both, although over the season Jonas got about twice as much field time as Wilkinson. Jonas played almost all of our two Ottawa games in September; and in the second game when Wilkinson came in during the third quarter and didn't do much, he was jeered. Jonas went all the way in our loss to Montreal. When he couldn't get anything started in Calgary I put Wilkinson in, but we still didn't score so I went back to Jonas for the entire second half. Then it was Wilkinson's turn, in that stunning game he played for us in Hamilton.

From the psychological standpoint, they were opposites. Although Jonas never gave me a moment's trouble with arguments or temperament, his feeling was that to be most effective he had to be the guy depended upon, the architect, designer, complete quarterback; to make mistakes, maybe, but to overcome them by great confidence. He is one of the toughest quarterbacks physically who ever lived. He was a tireless worker and would spend hours after practice running but he had to be doing the whole job himself or he didn't feel he was making his contribution.

Wilkinson was the opposite. He could adjust to anything. He didn't have the natural ability of Jonas but had a great knowledge of the game and had his own leadership qualities. He also had a couple of years' edge on Jonas in C.F.L. experience. In my overall plan, he was going to bring Jonas along far enough that Jonas could ultimately take over. It was a pretty healthy situation to have a guy like Wilkinson to bring Jonas along. But in Jonas' way of thinking he didn't have to be brought along. With him it was, You gotta throw me in there and I gotta get my feet wet and I gotta stay in there. And if you take me out it's like starting all over again.

There was no way in my mind that Jonas and Wilkinson were going to keep on alternating for the next ten years. I felt that Jonas would ultimately win because of his natural ability but I also felt that when that time came Wilkinson was a stable enough person that he could sit on the bench while Jonas was playing – and be there in emergencies. That was my plan although naturally at the time I kept it to myself.

After the Hamilton win we were on the right track again. Six days later Jonas played one of his best games for us, beating B.C. Lions 50-7. That put us past Hamilton into second place but they came back and beat Ottawa twice in five days and went ahead of us again. We were coming up to a game that I desperately wanted to win, for more reasons than just winning, which is usually enough. The two defeats by Montreal earlier in the season had been galling to me because each time Etcheverry went out of the park grinning and smoking his cigar while I fumed. And our next game was with Montreal. Before it we went through a little controversy with the commissioner's office again.

With Bobby Taylor still injured, we'd been using Jim Thorpe as flanker and he'd been playing well. But he hurt his knee in the B.C. game. The doctor said he needed an operation and would be gone for the season. I put in a hurry-up call for Billy Gambrell. I'd coached him at South Carolina and he'd turned pro with the St. Louis Cardinals and had some great years with them before being cut that year. I thought of him as a possibility for the following year besides being insurance in case Thorpe was really out. I found Gambrell at a construction job in California and he hopped a plane.

Thorpe was completely immobile for Monday and Tuesday of that week. Couldn't walk at all. Still, we were going to wait before putting him on the 30-day injury list to see how he came along.

Wednesday he came down to the stadium. He certainly wasn't ready to play. But with Gambrell in town and decisions to be made, I said, "Do you think you're going to be able to play in a week or so?"

He said, "I can play right now."

I said, "How can you play? You can hardly walk."

He said, "Watch me." And he proceeded to jump with both feet up and touch his toes, do deep knee bends and sprint up and down the inside of the stadium. The trainer, the doctor and everybody else was completely dumbfounded. To them, his knee was for all purposes gone.

When he came back he was still walking with a little bit of a limp. I hated to take a chance on playing him but I also didn't want to put him on the mandatory 30-day injury list. I could play Gambrell but I really didn't know how he'd go either.

I called Thorpe into my office. I said, "This is what we are going to have to do. You're going to tell me that there is no way that you're going to accept medical attention. Then I'm going to have to suspend you." A suspension could be lifted at any time, while he'd be out 30 days if we declared him injured.

He said, "Okay, I won't accept any medical attention."

So we sent word to the commissioner's office suspending Thorpe because he wouldn't accept medical attention. There was a big suspicion around the commissioner's office that this was a ploy and that Thorpe was all right. The commissioner called me about it.

I said, "Well, I know he wouldn't listen to the trainer and the doctor." Which was always true with Thorpe. "Why don't you get in touch with him and ask him? We'll see if we can have him call your office and give you his statement on what the hell the situation is."

So we did and about an hour later Thorpe called the commissioner's office.

"Mr. Gaudaur," he said. "This is Jim Thorpe. There is nobody going to fuss with my knee. I think I'm all right. I can cure myself. On my own behalf I'm just going to stay away and cure myself."

Jake said, "You know that if you do and they suspend you, you won't be paid."

"I know but I'm still not going to ruin my whole career over an operation," Thorpe said.

Jake called me back about ten minutes later and said, "Well, I just talked to him. He's suspended."

He was out for only a couple of games, a lot better than four. Against Montreal Gambrell caught six passes for 153 yards, including a long one that set up the winning touchdown. He might have scored it himself but not having played for a while he just plain got tuckered out and was caught. We beat Montreal 16-13 and I was the one with the cigar and the big grin that day. But in the next game Gambrell didn't play well at all. None of us did. We had a chance at first place that day but Hamilton beat us 27-7. A few days later in our last game of the season we beat Ottawa 19-17 to win second place. That brought us to the last disappointment of a generally disappointing season.

That was a game where Jonas really drew a blank; our semi-final with Etcheverry's Alouettes. Still, we were leading 7-6 in the last quarter when Sonny Wade on our 49-yard line threw Peter Dalla Riva a pass that was really no hell but Dalla Riva made a supernatural catch. He dove through the air and caught it falling flat on his belly button on our 17-yard line. From there they came out of the huddle and Wade ran the sprint-out pass and hit Tom Pullen for a touchdown. We go right back and have the same opportunity at the other end of the field, on the sprint-out pass. But Jonas missed Thorpe by inches. That touchdown would have won the game for us.

It was also the worst-officiated game I've ever seen. A few days later I got Hap Shouldice, the head of the officials, and asked him to review the films with me. He told me personally that it was the worst-officiated game he'd ever seen, too. So okay, they beat us 16-7. But at one stage of the game with us leading, we were on their one-yard line, third down. Symons went for it and was stopped. Their line coach, Bobby Ward, got a lot of attention for his defense on that play. But when you looked at the films, you saw something different. When the line of scrimmage is on the one, the defense cannot go beyond the goal-line, right? One yard away. It should have been the easiest thing in the world for the head linesman to see, straight along the goal line, that Steve Booras, their defensive end, had both hands six inches over the goal line. Both hands! And Mark Kosmos, playing linebacker on the left side, jumped to straddle the white line before the ball was snapped. That should have meant an automatic first down for the Argonauts on the one-yard line and we would have gone in to score and win it. Might even have won the Grey Cup, as Montreal did. Instead of that, when we were stopped and the Montreal offside wasn't called, they got the ball. But films don't win football games. "Son-of-a-bitch," I said at the end. Now we have to live with this all winter.

A Psychological Shock
Named Barrow

When I heard in January of 1971 that Toronto Argonauts were looking for a general manager to be my boss, I heard it from the newspapers: that John Bassett had nominated his son, Johnny F., and Len Lumbers, Jr., and Charles Burns' son, Michael, to conduct the search. I went to Lew Hayman and said, "What's this deal about hiring a general manager?"

Understand, he was president of the football club, chief executive officer. But he said, "I just heard about it myself. Somebody in the press called me and said, 'What to you think about it?' "

I thought it was a plain slap in the face to me. For five years, I'd been doing 95 per cent of the work. Lew represented the club at C.F.L. general managers' meetings. But I was in complete charge of the football program: recruiting and signing players and coaches, trades, keeping the negotiation list. The only other things a general manager would do with most football teams was a little public relations and administering the season ticket program. At the time, since I came, we'd gone from nothing to something on the field and from 13,500 season tickets to 29,000. "I've proven that I have ability as a general manager," I said. "I would have liked the opportunity of maybe turning the job down."

"I didn't have anything to do with it, Leo," Lew said. "But you're not a general manager type."

I said, "That's a goddam insult, why do you say that?"

"Not because you can't do it," he said. "I'm sure you can do it and I'm sure you would be good at it. But you'd vegetate. You've got to be on the firing line."

A year and a half later and partly as a result of this general manager situation, I was really going to find out what the firing line was.

I didn't pull any punches with reporters. I told them it was plain stupidity and damned rude, that I had to find out from the newspapers that Argos were looking for a general manager. In fact, I heard by the grapevine a little later that this g.m.-hunt was aimed at Lew, too. The young directors especially would look around and see Red O'Quinn doing this as general manager in Montreal and some other guy doing that elsewhere. Lew had said once or twice that he was going to retire. Meanwhile, some directors felt that he was drawing a lot of money for the work load he had and that hiring a general manager would be more efficient. Yet they didn't discuss the matter with him on a face-to-face confrontation basis. They chose the other way, much more of an insult to him, of going ahead without even letting him know.

When the word got out in headlines and sports columns that I was upset, Johnny Bassett, Jr. called me and said he and the other two wanted me to meet with them to discuss it. The meeting was in Lew Hayman's office. Johnny's mouth was so dry he couldn't spit. He was spokesman for the group. I've been friendly with him. He's a great competitor, plays good tennis and good squash and he's been a champion in his own right. So there has to be some substance to him as well as all the money and power. He wouldn't try to tell me a lot of plays from boarding school and how I should be handling personnel, like Mike Burns did. Of course, I never listened to Burns. I mean, once young Burns told me, dead serious, that I should try some of the plays he'd used in college. He also questioned whether certain players were giving 100 per cent. I knew who was and who wasn't, and didn't need advice on that score. I always thought that one reason owners hired a football coach was so they could allow their kids the time to learn their own business, instead of dabbling in coaching. Anyway, in those days and later, Mike Burns was drum major for the wrong people's band, as far as I was concerned. On the other hand, Len Lumbers, Jr., was a pretty down-to-earth gentleman-type person. I don't think he wanted too much part of nailing anybody to the cross. But he'd go along with the others.

Johnny's line was this: "The only reason we haven't considered you for the job is because you are our coach. We're satisfied with you as coach and we want to keep you there."

I told them I wasn't sure that I would accept the general managership if it was offered to me because my ambition was to coach in the Grey Cup. "But I would have liked you to wait until the end of the season before you made this move. Ultimately, I want to work up in this organization. If you hire another guy now, it ends any chance I'd have later."

They asked if I had any suggestions for candidates.

I said, "Yeah. Bill McPeak, from the Detroit Lions." Bill is a personal friend of mine. He'd been head coach of the Washington Redskins, had done a lot of football administrative work and was a hell of a guy. I called Bill McPeak. He said he'd be interested. They said they'd talk to him.

I found out later how that went. They flew Bill McPeak in from Detroit to the Toronto airport for an interview. Johnny Bassett wasn't there. Only Lumbers and Burns showed up. In the course of the conversation when McPeak was asking one thing and another, they told him he didn't have to be too concerned about Cahill because Cahill might not be around too long. This seemed like a slight contradiction to what Johnny had told me in our earlier meeting when he said how satisfied they were with my coaching.

McPeak told them, "Evidently you want to run the football team. If you want me as general manager I'll run the football team. I'll make the judgements on whether the coach should be fired or what should happen. If you want me on that basis, fine. If you want a yes man, I'm not your man."

He went back to Detroit. I heard later that the report to

Bassett was that Bill McPeak said he would be interested in the job but didn't want the front office work.

I asked McPeak about that a few days later. He said, "They're full of shit. I know what a general manager's job is. I wouldn't make any foolish trip to Toronto to talk about a general manager's job if I didn't want to assume the responsibility of front office work."

Then he added, "But I'm going to tell you something right now, Leo. You're on bad ground. You're associated with. . . ." Well, I wouldn't want to quote exactly what he called them. Not good. "These guys are after you," he said. "They don't know anything about football but they're going to try to get you."

Meanwhile, they had been talking to other people. Many names were mentioned in the press. Dick Shatto, who'd been a great Argo player before my time, was interested. Johnny Bassett talked to Jim Finks, the Minnesota Vikings general manager, who'd worked in Calgary earlier. Johnny did say that wasn't a job offer but a request for advice. Rogers Lehew, the Calgary general manager, was another they investigated but he wouldn't be free until mid-summer on his Calgary contract. Also, John Barrow's name began to be mentioned. But I simply couldn't believe that was serious.

In the first four years I was with the Argos, Barrow was in his last four of 14 years as a lineman with Hamilton Tiger-Cats. He'd come from the University of Florida in 1956, by-passed the Detroit Lions who'd made him a third draft choice, signed with the Tiger-Cats and became a Canadian citizen in 1961. He was an All-Canadian lineman for 11 years in a row. Still, that doesn't qualify a man to be a general manager, even in Hamilton. But to imagine Argos looking toward a Hamilton football player when they wanted a general manager, you have to able to imagine that Pierre Trudeau would try to get Robert Stanfield into his cabinet, or that President Nixon would ask Ted Kennedy in to clean up the White House.

I don't give a damn what the public might think of such

things; that it's all business, etc., and if a guy is qualified it doesn't matter where he's been. That's okay for selling cars or neckties. But football is an emotional, physical game where hatreds rise fast and don't die down easily. To understand what it was like between Hamilton and Toronto, you'd have to be an Argonaut coach or player. All we'd ever heard at the start in 1967 was wait until the Tigers roar. They start slow but they come fast towards the end of the year. All that stuff. All I know is that from 1967 until 1972 they were still coming. In 1967, Ralph Sazio's last as coach, I think he managed to beat my football team, which was in a formative stage, in three games by nine points or something like that. In '68, '69, '70, and '71 we changed the whole atmosphere. We made these guys believe that it was not Hamilton that would come at the end of the season but Toronto. This beat-Hamilton thing was the strongest football emotion I'd felt in Canada. My criterion for a great football team was one with which I could feel comfortable getting off the bus in Hamilton.

I've stood on the sidelines in Hamilton and heard the remarks and felt the pressure and the electricity in the stands that came from 50 years of Toronto and Hamilton playing football, and mouthed a prayer of thanks that I had an opportunity to be part of such a hell of a fight. The bitterness that is born out of a sports contest should be forgotten after the contest is over but in the Toronto-Hamilton thing it was almost hatred. I loved that feeling, I loved that challenge and I just couldn't imagine that anyone could ever consider going into that atmosphere, take somebody from Hamilton and make him my boss.

So when I heard rumors that Barrow had applied for the job, I laughed them off. I said, "There is no way Barrow's going to get it." Especially Barrow. He'd made caustic remarks about our football team which naturally an opposing player might do – but there they were, they were remembered. The same guys he'd bad-mouthed as a player, including me, were still the guys Argos depended on. Added to that, in his last years as a football player he wasn't playing very well. He was just hanging in there. A lot of our players had even less respect for him than he did for them.

Still, people kept telling me it was just possible, that Argonauts had done things in the past that defied all reason. I still said no, and this was reinforced when John Bassett said in my presence that Barrow would be our general manager only over his dead body.

When he finally was named to the job I went home to Shirley and said, "Shirley, if someone did a research program asking the most eminent scientists in the world, 'How can Argonauts screw up this operation?' somewhere in a secret laboratory would be a little guy with thick glasses, the outstanding scientist of all time. After reams and reams of calculations and equations and everything else he would come to the conclusion that the only way Argonauts could screw themselves up was to go to Hamilton and get a defensive lineman out of a three-point stance to be the captain of the good ship Argonaut." And I said, "That's what they've done." She was as amazed as I was.

My father taught me all my life, "Look, make the best of things. If you can't do that, back out, or go elsewhere, but don't muddy the waters. After something is done, don't be an architect of disaster. Do the right thing."

So I told Shirley also that there was nothing for me to do but quit or put up with it. My ambition was to go to the Grey Cup. At this stage I thought the only way I could get there was just try to get along with the guy.

People tell me that on the day Barrow's appointment was announced in Bassett's office, I was pale. That was a tremendous understatement of how I felt. I stood there while John Bassett told the reporters and TV cameras, "We agreed that before the coach moves on to more responsible positions in football, he wants to bring the Grey Cup to Toronto. . . . So I took Mr. Cahill out of the ball game early." Meaning in the seach for a g.m. Then I said a few words confirming what he'd said. That was April 22nd, 1971. Later I met Barrow for lunch and told him exactly how I felt. We simply agreed that he would do his job and I would do mine.

I tried to put it all out of my mind and get on with the job but there were constant distractions. In Hamilton they were laughing about how they had to send somebody over to Toronto to run our football team. People at the Argonaut Rowing Club told me they were appalled that this guy from Hamilton would be sitting there saying football in Toronto was all screwed up and that the Hamilton attitude had to prevail. These people said, "Christ, doesn't he realize that he's talking in the Argonaut Rowing Club? Where the football team originally came from?" They used to buy him scotch and water just to have him talk and then they'd pick up the phone and call me and say, "Can you imagine him saying stuff like this?"

For the first year the idea was that Barrow wouldn't take much part in the football team but would be around, learning the ropes. But he had in his mind, right from the start, where this was going to lead. Maybe it could be traced back to the impression Bill McPeak got from Burns and Lumbers before he warned me. Anyway, early in 1973 Barrow told a TV broadcaster, who told me, that the minute he signed with the Argos I was as good as gone.

Secrets of Recruiting
the Big Ones

Charlie Sanders, tight end with Detroit Lions, may not know it but he taught me a lot about recruiting quality football players. By quality I mean people so good that we have to fight for them all the way with the National Football League. If you want to do it successfully without going overboard financially, you have to have some ingenuity and some ability and sometimes you also have to be a tough son-of-a-bitch. At least a couple of times when we were signing U.S. college stars to Toronto contracts in the spring of 1971, I had something to thank Charlie Sanders for.

He taught me the lesson back in 1968 and I'd honed it up a little since. The way I did it in 1968, I was strictly Charlie Sanders' benefactor. I gave him cards to play with.

I needn't go into the early details but late in the chase we felt we just about had him. Blackie had been on the University of Minnesota campus talking to him. I was in the airport at Chicago with Herb Solway, pursuing someone else, but I got Charlie on the phone for a final discussion of exactly what we were offering. His agent, Jim Morse of Muskegon, Michigan, was with him. I spelled it out: salary, bonuses, fringes, with Herb standing right beside me. When Charlie and Jim Morse both agreed that they'd accept it I said, "Wait a minute. I want to put my lawyer on and you tell him exactly what it is you understand the deal is, so there won't be any hitches later." Herb squeezed into the phone booth probably thinking they'd never told him about this kind of practice at law school. Yep, they had it all straight.

But Herb was suspicious. When he came off the phone he said, "I think you should fly there and sign him right now."

What? Was he suggesting a football player might go back on his word? Never! And some won't, either, but it's prudent not to tempt them. Anyway, I didn't go. Right there I was committing the cardinal sin, letting him loose with my detailed offer, so that his agent could call Detroit, which had drafted him third, and bargain: "Well, Toronto is willing to pay him this and that. . . . " Whereupon Detroit would say, as I would in their place with a guy like that, a potential star: Don't sign a thing, we'll match it and do better.

When I got home I had trouble raising Mr. Sanders to get the signing completed. I sent Blackie to Minnesota. He called me to say that Sanders and Morse were flying out of Minnesota and he was getting on the same plane. There were some comic interludes before Blackie arrived with them in Muskegon where Morse's home was. When he got there, he was right in Morse's house by then, he phoned me and said Morse wanted to take Sanders to Detroit the next day.

I said, "Christ, the guy agreed." So Morse got on the phone and said, "I feel it is my responsibility to take this kid to Detroit."

I called him a lying son-of-a-bitch and everything else I could think of. But Blackie called me in the morning and said, "They're going to Detroit."

I said, "Get in the car and go with them."

Morse had a big Cadillac. Charlie Sanders and Morse were in the front seat, Blackie in the back, smoking a cigar. Now, envision this. They pull up in front of the Detroit Lions office and go in, but leave Blackie outside. In the office they'd got Night Train Lane and other Detroit stars to talk to Charlie Sanders. What a way to negotiate. All Morse had to do was open the venetian blinds and say, "There's the Toronto coach, waiting in the car. This is what we want. . . . " They signed him right there with Blackie in the back seat of the car outside. And of course Charlie Sanders became the best tight end in the N.F.L. I'd had Charlie Sanders completely committed to a contract – but only verbally. By letting him get away without signing I'd handed all the negotiating power to the other team where they could go one dollar better or offer a new car or some other thing.

That taught me, and it stood me in good stead later – like early in 1971 with Jim Stillwagon of Ohio State. We'd known of him, as everybody in football did, from when he was a junior and was selected on most of the major All-America teams as middle guard. We put him on our negotiation list then. In his senior year he repeated all those awards, made the *Look* magazine All-Americans, was picked by the college coaches as Lineman of the Year for the Vince Lombardi Block of Granite award, and also won the Knute Rockne trophy as the nation's best lineman. There were dozens of other awards. I think he was the most honored lineman in football history. While he was still playing, we didn't make a nuisance of ourselves, but called him from time to time to let him know our interest. Any more direct approaches while he was still in college would have annoyed his coach, Woody Hayes, who might have hurt our chances of getting him eventually. But once the 1970 season was over, and the 1971 Rose Bowl – his second – and the Hula Bowl, I called him at his home and invited him to come to Toronto and see us. There was also an offensive guard, Stillwagon's roommate, who wanted to play professional football. I invited him as well so that Stillwagon wouldn't come into town cold but would have some company.

It is funny how things happen. We took them out to dinner at Bardi's, across from the Royal York Hotel, and introduced them to different players and also he met some of the Argo old guard, players of 15 or 20 years ago like Rod Smylie and Doug Smylie and others, guys who knew his reputation, to let him see he was just as well known in Canada as he was in the U.S. But we couldn't be with him all the time. On the second day, I think it was, I gave him $50 spending money and suggested they go out on their own and take a look at the town.

They were having a beer in this place. The waitress came and served them their beer off a tray. Stillwagon gave her a bill and she gave him some change. He took a quarter and flipped it up onto the tray. He was just doing it as a tip, you know, a kind of a gesture. But it lit in a dish of spaghetti and caused a goddam uproar in the place. The manager came over and asked Stillwagon to leave. When he told me later, I realized that it was the kind of a thing we could have lost him over – for a player of his status to be treated rudely over a silly thing like that. That's not the way to recruit a football player. But we'd done the important selling job earlier, I guess, on the team itself and the hunting and fishing in Ontario and opportunities for a job outside of football.

When they left to go back to Ohio State, Stillwagon told me, "I'll let you know on Thursday what I decide." We'd talked money and other terms. I said, "Okay, I'd appreciate that."

Before he came to Toronto he had talked to Green Bay, which had drafted him fifth and intended to use him as a middle linebacker. I knew Green Bay's M.O. was much like that of the rest of the teams in the National Football League. They know that there are going to be five or six meetings before they ultimately sign a kid. So on their first meeting they usually low-play him and his accomplishments in college. Now this guy had won every title that a lineman can win. But when he went to Green Bay I just knew they'd tell him, Look, you haven't played a minute of professional football, you've got a little bit of a height problem (he's six feet, which is short for an N.F.L. linebacker), and so on. They say these things just so the guy doesn't hit them with a hundred thousand dollar contract demand right away. They underplay him, then let him cool off and then talk to him again and build the price up a little. I knew I'd caught him right after this first meeting. I could sense a kind of disenchantment with that they'd told him at Green Bay.

He'd said he would let me know on Thursday. I got real

edgy on Wednesday. Something told me that everything wasn't going right. I called his apartment in Columbus, Ohio. His friend answered the phone, the one he'd brought up with him. I'd offered him a contract, too.

I said, "Have you sent in your contract yet?"

He said, "Yeah, Coach. I got it signed and it's in the mail."

I said, "Between you and me, what's 'Wagon going to do?" He said that was between us and he didn't think he ought to get into that. I told him he wouldn't be revealing anything, that he was an Argonaut now and I'd appreciate it if he'd let me know anything I should know.

He said, "Well, between us, I think he's going to stiff you. I heard him talking to Green Bay and he's made arrangements to go up there on Saturday."

I said, "Damnit, he is going to let me know tomorrow what he is going to do and he's already made arrangements to go to Green Bay on Saturday? That doesn't sound right."

I thought about it and thought about it. I woke up at six the next morning and got on the phone to Gordie Ackerman. I told him to get on a plane, go to Columbus, find Stillwagon, then call me back.

He didn't ask any questions. I waited in my office through lunch and into the afternoon. I was getting nervous. At three o'clock Gordie called and said, "I've been all over this campus, at the football office, his apartment and his girl friend's place, into the gym, every place. I can't find him."

I said, "Well, damn, he's gotta be there some place unless he's gone to Green Bay already." Just then Brenda, my secretary, came in and said, "Scott Knisley is on the other phone." That was a lawyer in Columbus who really doesn't take a piece of the action but helps some kids.

I said, "Gordie, hold on." I pushed the hold button and picked up the other line. Scott said, "Coach, Jim Stillwagon is here in my office right now, with the assistant athletic director from Ohio State. We want to know what your offer is."

I said I had a coach probably within a couple of miles of

him right then. "Give me your address. I'll have him come over and be with you when we talk about our offer." He gave me the address and I picked up the other phone and said, "Gordie, this is where they are and this is what I want you to do. Go over there and make sure that you don't let them out of the room after I propose what I'm going to propose. This is the way we are going to do it. I'm going to give them a figure. When I give them the figure, they are going to tell you yes or no. You've got the contracts right there. Hang tough with me on this thing."

So he said okay and left for Scott Knisley's office and in a few minutes I called Scott back and outlined our offer: salary, bonus, the works. "How does that sound?"

He said, "That sounds pretty good. I'll tell him." As if he was going to hang up.

I said, "Just a moment, Scott. There is one other contingency here. Pat Peppler, the assistant general manager at Green Bay, is a personal friend of mine. I know he's been talking to Stillwagon. I just want you to know one thing. This is our final offer. This is as far as we will go. I want Stillwagon to tell me right now yes or no. I've already instructed my coach there with you that there won't be any phone calls to Green Bay or anything else before we get an answer. I just want to know from Stillwagon, standing on his own two feet in terms of what I've told you, what the answer is." .

He said, "Well, what the hell! You're not giving us a chance to get back to Green Bay."

"You've been to Green Bay already. Now you know our offer, too. If you say no, I've got Pat Peppler's number right here and I'm picking up the phone and telling him we're out of it. We've got Stillwagon on our negotiation list. Nobody else in Canada can touch him. But if he doesn't want to go along with the contract we're offering, we're out of it and you can settle with Green Bay for whatever they want to offer you."

Gordie told me later Scott went over to Stillwagon, outlined the offer and said, "They're being fair with you. I don't think you should sign it until you get back from Green Bay, but they say you have to say yes or no to the contract right now. If you say no, they're calling Green Bay and telling them they're completely out of the thing."

I gambled that Green Bay had shot lower than us on their original bid. But anyway Stillwagon had to make up his mind that if he said no, and we were out of it, he had to take what Green Bay offered on his hands and knees.

He said, "Give me the pen. I'm signing."

If he had been able to get back to Green Bay, they'd have matched it or gone better. But Charlie Sanders long before had shown me the error of letting that happen. When you can chase a guy with Stillwagon's talent, compete with the N.F.L., get his trust and get his name on the contract, you've done a great job of recruiting. It isn't like going out with a basket full of money and paying a guy $50,000 more than the National Football League would pay, which is the misconception many people have about the Argonauts. They just don't know. Better still, in that Grey Cup year Stillwagon lived up to everything. He was all-world as far as I was concerned.

We had three other major jobs of recruiting that spring. Two were in competition with the N.F.L. One I sometimes wished later I hadn't won, but we'll get to that – and I'm not referring to Leon McQuay.

The big pressure from the directors was to get a new quarterback. I wasn't trading the ones I had until I had something better. But we were very active in the quarterback market all winter. We tried for Gary Beban and that didn't work out. We played some long-range footsie with Russ Jackson on the rumor that he might unretire if the price was right, but I don't think he was really serious. That brought us down to two, Joe Theismann of Notre Dame and Greg Barton of Detroit Lions.

We first started watching Joe Theismann in earnest in the spring of 1970. He had had a great 1969 season, ending with a win in the Cotton Bowl. Blackie Johnston and Jim Rountree were making the rounds of the Big Ten spring camps. When they got to South Bend, Indiana, they saw him in practice. They called me right away. Jim told me, "This kid has the quickest feet I ever saw. Let's put him on our negotiation list." We did. Most of his college awards came in 1970, including setting a dozen Notre Dame records and being runner-up to Stanford's Jim Plunkett for the Heisman trophy.

During that season we called him from time to time to say hello. I went to South Bend for Notre Dame's game with Georgia Tech and met him for the first time in the dressing room after. I just introduced myself, repeated our interest in him and saw for the first time the sparkle in his eye. I knew he was a buyer, not a shopper, the kind of guy who would make things happen. Later there was his tremendous performance in the Cotton Bowl when Notre Dame upset number one-ranked Texas. Joe passed for one touchdown and ran for two more in the first 16 minutes of that game.

When he came back from the Hula Bowl in January I went to South Bend two or three times, took him out to dinner, met his wife. My pitch to him was how much better I thought he could do in Canada than anywhere else. Miami had drafted him but the competition there was tough. Bob Griese was young and seemed to have the job well in hand. We talked about Joe's future. Joe is smart and mature. With him it went beyond the I, the perpendicular pronoun thing, to thinking about his wife and family. Still there was the glamor of Miami and the N.F.L. appealing to him.

So I laid the groundwork and in the meantime the directors were getting pretty excited about him, too. In February or early March he was brought into Toronto by Jack Carmichael, a sports buff who owns a car dealership, City Buick. This was to attend a party where Joe would meet the directors of the football team. I was out of the city recruiting someone else. Joe's first concrete offer from Argonauts came that day, from Bassett himself, with all those other people around. It impressed him, as it was meant to do, that he was up here in that kind of a high level group. But after that, even with the great influence that they brought to bear on this kid, he had to consider the N.F.L.

On March 17th, he and his wife, Sheri, flew to Miami for I guess what Miami coach Don Shula would consider the clincher.

We knew about their trip but still had hopes because Bassett's offer had been a good one. However, I got a call that next afternoon, March 18, from Sheri. She said she just wanted to tell me that Joe had signed with Miami Dolphins. She said Joe was still in the press conference with Don Shula but she and Joe both wanted to let me know right away, before I heard it elsewhere.

I told her that whatever Joe did I knew that he was going to be a great success and a great football player and I wished them both well, and wished we could have had them with us in Toronto. I laid it on and meant every word of it because they are such fine kids. Funny, Joe reflected on my reaction that day once when we talked later. He said, "You know, Sheri told me, 'I really hated to say goodbye to Coach Cahill because he's been so nice to us about the whole thing.' "

When the newspapers carried a story from Miami on March 19 with the headline "Theismann a Dolphin", I thought that was that with Joe. It made me try that much harder to get Greg Barton nailed down. Greg had a good college career at Tulsa and was drafted by Detroit in 1968 but hadn't got off the taxi squad much, with Greg Landry and Bill Munson ahead of him. He was a friend of Angelo Mosca, the Hamilton player, and it was from Mosca we first got the word that Greg might be available to us. We put him on our negotiation list. Also Jim Martin, on the Detroit coaching staff, is a friend of Blackie Johnston's. He told Blackie he thought Barton was a hell of a football player. Blackie went to see him and was impressed. Barton had played out his option with Detroit in 1970 and, under the N.F.L. contract provisions, would become a free agent on May 1, 1971.

I had Barton to Toronto for a couple of days at the Royal York. Blackie and I and our wives had dinner with him. He seemed to know a lot about Canadian football from playing at Tulsa for Glen Dobbs, once a coach and star quarterback for

Saskatchewan, and from watching it on TV in Detroit. We were impressed.

I talked to Chuck Knox in Florida early in 1971. Knox was an assistant at Detroit at the time, before he went to the L.A. Rams as head coach. I mentioned Barton's name. He said, "I know you've snuck in here and taken some draft choices away from the N.F.L. but don't ball us up on Barton. As a personal favor. We've got plans for him." I soon found out what he meant. Philadelphia was after Barton. They had let their number one quarterback, Norm Snead, go to Minnesota and traded three high draft choices to Detroit for Barton, gambling that he'd go where he was sure of playing. They were really counting on him big. There was a new stadium in Philadelphia, the chance to be the big guy there. They put a lot of pressure on him, but we felt we still had a chance. We arranged a meeting with Barton I think for March 26 in Indianapolis, a week after Miami announced it had signed Theismann. Barton hadn't yet come to his option date, when he'd be free to sign, so this meet had to be secret. We picked Indianapolis because none of us would likely be recognized there. Herb Solway and I got on a plane and flew down. I needed Herb because Charlie Dubin, the team lawyer, was away in Ottawa on business.

We got into the hotel one evening, had a drink with Barton, and made arrangements to meet at a lawyer's office the following day. That's when we really got down to specifics. As we came closer and closer to agreement, Barton sat over in the corner of the room by himself. When he was queried about this or that, his one remark was, "Shoot, all I want to do is play." When we got down to the point where we were all agreed, we were on touchy ground. We could not have a valid contract until May 1 because it wouldn't really stand up legally until then, when his option date was up. So really any time between then and May 1 the only strength that I had would be Barton's word. He wouldn't take any money until after May 1 when a contract could become legal. But anyway, when we went back to Toronto we felt that even though we'd missed on Theismann, we now had one quarterback in the bank.

Now enters Jack Carmichael again, the City Buick man who'd brought Theismann to Toronto the first time. Football buffs of this kind aren't always a help but some are – with contacts on a business basis around the country. He had a deal going with someone in South Bend, another well-off business man. A day or two after our meeting with Barton, Carmichael was making a call to his friend in South Bend. Theismann's name was mentioned. The man said, "Incidentally, Joe's right here with me now. We're having a drink to toast him going to Miami."

Carmichael said, "Let me talk to him. I want to give him my congratulations and best wishes." In the subsequent conversation, Jack thought Joe didn't sound completely sure he was making the right move. Jack phoned to tell me this impression.

I called Joe and learned that he had signed the Miami contract, all right, but hadn't mailed it because he didn't have a stamp. He asked if I could send our contract from Toronto to him so that he could compare one more time.

I said, "Joe, we've gone through this. I know Don Shula and the Miami situation and there is no way I'm going to send our contract so that you have both our contract and theirs." But I could see the opening. "If you feel this way," I said, "Well, Sheri has never seen Toronto. If there's any doubt in your mind you owe it to yourself and Sheri to come up and sit down one last time and read our contract over with your wife."

He agreed to fly in on the following Sunday. Herb Solway and I went to the airport to meet them. We tried to show Sheri the best of the city. We drove south on Highway 27 to the Lakeshore and downtown, then up through good residential areas to the Bayview area where Herb lives. I thought it would be a good idea to have Sheri meet Herb's family as sort of a third-party influence. We went in and introduced Sheri to Elaine Solway and had a social drink. About then, Herb called John Bassett (they are personal friends) to let him know the Theismanns were there. In a little while Bassett dropped in for a minute. His little girl was with him and his wife was in the car, I think. Bassett came in and said, "I just wanted to say hello and shake hands again, Joe, and meet your wife and tell you that we hope that we will have you here." A few more words and then he said goodbye and left us to it.

After another few minutes, business. I said, "Joe, I want to go over this contract and what we have to offer you one more time." I took him in a little study off the living room. Sheri stayed with Elaine. They had lots to talk about. Joe and I went point by point over the whole contract. He's an honorable kid and I'm sure he felt that he had almost a commitment with Miami. But he wanted to do the right thing, not only for himself but for his family. And I concentrated very strongly on that. I told him, "If it was only you and I was in your position, I'd go definitely to Miami and take my best shot. But if you want to think about future security, the kind of outside career you can build here, and the overall picture of your family, Toronto's offer is much better."

I also told him that if he signed with us, he would definitely play. After two years were up, he could still decide on whether to stay in Canada or have a shot at the N.F.L. I emphasized that his performance in Toronto would enhance his status as an N.F.L. prospect, whatever he decided on eventually. This seemed to appeal to him.

At the end I told him, "What I want you to do now is go over this contract with Sheri. Take time and go over it carefully. Then come out and we'll talk about what you've decided."

When I left he took Sheri into the den. They walked out at the end of 30 minutes or so. The first thing Sheri said was, "Well, we can always go to Miami on a visit." Meaning that after she'd seen the contract in black and white she'd made up her mind. Joe came out behind her. He wasn't as definite yet. Time was getting short. We had to get them back soon to catch the plane back to South Bend.

All of a sudden Joe turned to me and said, "Coach, let me take the contract home tonight to South Bend. I'll sit down with

Sheri again and we'll go over this thing. I'll let you know tomorrow."

"No way," I said. "You've gone over the Miami contract, you've shown it to your wife, and you've both gone over our contract. You know right now what you want to do. If you want to go to Miami, like I said before, I wish you both luck. But if you want to stay in Toronto, now is the time to make your decision. Now is the time to sign."

He said, "Give me the pen." I happened to have a pen. He signed the contract.

In a day or so, April 5, it came out in the papers. Miami couldn't believe it. The air was blue down there. Bassett was quoted as saying the contract was in the safe and that the Toronto offer always had been better than Miami's financially. A total of about $200,000 over three years was mentioned. I always feel that contract amounts should be kept private; they're not mine to divulge. I didn't divulge that figure. But it was published. I never heard it denied. Joe said in South Bend that "money and security" convinced him and that "the simple point of the matter is that I changed my mind, Sunday."

So now we had four quarterbacks – Theismann, Barton (to come later), Jonas, and Wilkinson. I'd had my orders in no uncertain terms about trading Jonas and Wilkinson. If we hadn't both Theismann and Barton coming I would have put up a fight for Jonas. The same way I did when I wanted to keep Wilkinson and trade Gabler. But with Barton and Theismann signed, I was willing to go along, keep the upper echelon happy.

The Barton deal wasn't quite over. Late in April, about the time I traded Wilkinson to B.C., I had a call from Barton's agent, Chuck Barnes. He was calling from California, where he and Barton lived, and where a lot of wheels from the Philadelphia Eagles had been visiting lately, talking to Barnes and Barton.

He said, "Leo, I hate to tell you but we've decided to go to Philadelphia."

"Like hell you have, Chuck," I said. "Let me talk to Barton." I appealed to his honor in living up to the arrangements we'd agreed on in Indianapolis.

After a little pause, he said, "Okay, Coach, I'll come."

Right at that time Jerry Williams and other Philadelphia guys were out in California putting the pressure on him. May 1 was getting closer and they wanted to be sure they had a deal. Things were pretty hot. I guess Barnes had told Philly okay before he phoned me and then had to back off. It seemed not a bad idea after a while to put Barton where he couldn't be reached for comment but we couldn't come out in the open yet on it at all. We figured out a secret way to get some money to him. He and his wife went to Hawaii and were incommunicado. Nobody else knew where they were. On May 1 or thereabouts we filed his contract with the C.F.L. office. Philadelphia earlier had accused us of tampering. They claimed he'd agreed to terms with them verbally. On May 10, the N.F.L. said it was investigating a story that Toronto offered Barton a deal on March 26, which we had. On June 10, Jake Gaudaur and Commissioner Pete Rozelle of the N.F.L. agreed there was no academic proof of tampering. Case closed.

Life with Leon McQuay

There was a lot of talk in 1972, the second year we had Leon McQuay, that I gave him too much special consideration. Let him get away with too much. Was always giving him a break instead of kicking him in the ass. Not many people seemed to realize that his treatment in 1971 had been exactly the same but then he was fit, running for something like 960 yards in the first nine games and getting another 323 on passes, so far ahead of every other ball carrier in Canada that he was out of sight.

Frankly, I did give him special consideration. He is a special man, a greater football player than most coaches are ever exposed to in a lifetime. I didn't go busting my ass around the United States to sign exceptional football players and then treat them in a way that made them want to get the hell back home. I gave everybody special treatment of a sort, right down to the 32nd man on our football team. Whether a guy was old and wise like Dave Mann, or young and secure like Corrigall or Theismann, I treated each individual in accordance with his character and personality. Hell, with Bobby Taylor I looked the other way for years. As I used to tell them, "When we sat down and talked contract I can't ever remember telling you what I was going to do for someone else. It was always what I was going to do for you." For a mature professional, that's enough. We put something together in Toronto based on guys that we signed in hot competition with the N.F.L. And in the time I was there, following my way of doing things, we never lost one of them back to the U.S. Symons could have gone to the N.F.L. after his 1968 season. We simply didn't lose the guys that other clubs did, like Jake Scott at Miami, Bo Scott in Cleveland, Vic Washington, Joe Kapp, Margene Adkins, and many others who played in Canada at one time.

With Leon it started with the recruiting, early in 1971, about the same time we were pursuing Theismann. Leon then was not quite 21, a kid born and raised in a black neighborhood in Tampa – who had shown earlier in his life that he wanted to stay with his own people. When he came out of high school, colleges from all over the U.S. were hammering on his door. Everybody wanted him. Fran Curci was the coach then at the University of Tampa, a mile from Leon's home. At the height of the recruiting, Fran took him into his own home and had him live there for a while, to help get Leon to trust him. Because of this personal contact, Leon was able to stay right at home and play at the University of Tampa, their first black player. This was a big experience with the kid and he had great seasons with Tampa: 3,039 yards rushing and 37 touchdowns without even playing his senior year. Then Curci, whom he trusted and who'd told him, You come with me and we're going to make a football player out of you, had an opportunity to go to the University of Miami. He left. Curci offered to take Leon to the University of Miami, but that way by college football rules he'd have to extend his education and sit out a whole year before he was eligible to play again. The kid was thinking, What am I going to do? Where am I going to turn?

By then he's telling a couple of his buddies. They got to Ken Brown, who'd been with me at Montreal and now was a TV sports director in Orlando. Ken told me that Leon was very unhappy and wanted to get into professional football but wasn't eligible for the N.F.L. draft, again by football rules, until after his class graduated a year later. That's to prevent the N.F.L. from raiding colleges. But it doesn't apply to Canadian football. We had him on our negotiation list and were very interested in him.

I talked with Leon on the phone. He said, Sure, he'd like to talk about playing in Canada. I didn't feel a real obligation to Tampa University. The coach who had talked him into going to the University of Tampa and promised him some things had left him high and dry. Also, that stuff about, "How can you disrupt a kid's education?" – that's hogwash. That's the kind of argument that's fine for the University of Tampa or University of Illinois or any other school, to say you owe us because you came to our school on a scholarship. He doesn't owe them anything. He's paid them in full through his work on the football team each year for everything they invested in him. If I'd felt that Leon playing professional football in Canada would hurt his opportunity to graduate I would have second thoughts about the thing. But actually he could come up here and play professional football and go back to Tampa in the off-season with good money to attend semesters from January to June. It would take him maybe another year to graduate but he could live a college life that he never dreamed was possible; nice apartment, a chance to concentrate on his studies without being over-tired because of athletics.

So he agreed to come to Toronto to look around. He brought a girl friend with him who he was thinking about marrying. We spent some time together. He was difficult kid to communicate with. He wasn't sure of me or the situation. I know just what was going through his head. Leon, like a lot of young athletes, had been exploited because of his ability. It had been an experience for him to be the first black player in Tampa, going to college that was 95 per cent white, being the football superstar. But he realized he'd never been noticed or considered by the white population until all of a sudden he got all this publicity. Then everybody was interested in him. It was natural for him to suspect that if it wasn't for his football ability these people wouldn't be that interested. When a coach from Canada talked to him he felt the same way: if I go to Canada, to a strange country, with a strange coach, would this guy like me, above and beyond the fact that I'm a good football player?

What happens to me if I get hurt? Is this the kind of a guy that I want to take a chance on jeopardizing my career in the National Football League for? All these questions were on his mind.

When I was talking to him his concern was: "Where will I live? Can you pick me up in the morning and take me to practice? This is a big city." Real basic things. Maybe if the other Toronto players had known a little about this they'd have had more understanding later for the individual and what he was going through. When a lot of people talked about Leon's immaturity, it wasn't immaturity any more for him than it would be for any other kid his age to feel that way. He had a couple of extra reasons for feeling a little bit more protective about his situation is all.

I took all these things into consideration. I think he started to trust me. But I couldn't be sure. I thought that maybe with a kid like him, who hadn't been exposed to much money, a show of money would impress him. I went out and got ten thousand dollars' worth of hundred dollar bills. I carried them around in my pocket. In one of my final sessions with him I sat down across the table from him and I said, "Leon, I can right now give you ten thousand dollars as a down payment on your contract."

"That's an awful lot of money," he said. I thought I really had the clout then. His eyes opened up a little bit. I reached into my pocket and pulled out some hundreds and laid them on the table in front of him.

He said, "I don't want to touch that, 'cause if I touch it you will never get it back."

"Go ahead. It's yours if you want to sign with us right now."

He said, "No. I'm not going to take that money. There are a lot of things I'd like to have, and a lot of things I'd like to do. But I'll let you know Tuesday what I'm going to do."

He was extremely intelligent about that. It took a certain kind of good individual to turn his back on ten thousand dollars right then. It told me what a basically sound person he was.

He flew back to Tampa telling me he'd let me know Tuesday. Tuesday came about four times in a row and I never heard from him. I thought, Well the kid decided to go back to school. We fired our best shot. In my own assessment right then, he wanted to play professional football and liked me but didn't like Toronto enough to leave Tampa where he had been born and raised.

I called a contact in Florida and asked him to go to Tampa and find out what Leon was thinking. He talked to Leon and reported that Leon had some interest in coming back to Toronto for another look. I felt then we could sign him. But I also felt one element was missing – a third party, neutral, whom he could trust. I thought of a good agent named Tony Razzano. He's the agent for some good ones in the N.F.L., including Franco Harris who is wowing them now in Pittsburgh.

I called Tony and said, "Have you ever heard of Leon McQuay?" He said he had. "A good football player," he said. Tony wanted to know first if Leon had really decided to quit school. I told him of our earlier contacts and asked if he'd go to Tampa, talk to him and tell him the pros and cons of our offer. I said, "We're not kidding or deceiving him. We'll gamble that if he signs with Toronto he'll want to stay here. But at the end of two years, a one-year contract and the option year, he'll have pro experience, command a bigger bonus and be a more mature football player. We hope he'll stay forever but even if he doesn't, the years that he will have spent in Toronto he'll make good money. If he wants to go on in college he can go in the off-season and finish his education."

Tony said, "I'll fly down and talk to him."

That was what was needed: the outside opinion. Leon came to believe in Tony. This was the beginning of a marriage that has been very satisfactory. Still, it was a tough, long, hard, drawn-out effort. There was a lot of pressure put on Leon by the alumni at Tampa. That it was his responsibility to stay, being a black player and Tampa's first one. But Leon came to Toronto again and we made a future date to meet down in

Dayton, Ohio, at Tony's home. This was about the second week in May. At the last minute I called Tony. He said he hadn't heard from Leon. We thought maybe we were being stood up. But by the time I got to Tony's house, Leon was there. We sat around Tony's den. Leon never was much for drinking and doesn't smoke much. Tony and I had a couple of martinis while we talked a little more. I think Leon felt a belonging by then, belonging to me as a coach and to Tony as an adviser and agent. I don't think without Tony Razzano I could have handled things.

From when I announced his signing in Toronto on May 13, I wondered a lot of the time how I was going to handle Leon McQuay. I didn't know at that time what a perfectionist he was, what pride he had, how he could brood when things weren't going right. When he got in for training camp I tried to check with him as much as I could without interfering with his private life. I always left my door open any time he wanted to come in and see me. He was a loner, sometimes standoffish and rude, in the dressing room. Dave Raimey, who'd been the same route himself, was closer to him than anyone. I just wanted things to go right for Leon. I'd been close to him, talked to him, knew how he felt about his family, the closeness he had with his mother.

As time went on and he electrified every field he played on, he also built up his own reputation for being a problem child. The tantrums the ordinary football player has aren't nearly as magnified as those of the outstanding football player. He's in the public eye. Always they want to look at him, see how he dresses, how he acts, how he walks. If he limps a little more than most players or throws his helmet down a little oftener it is noticed more. He was hard to handle. I admit it.

The word started to get out in the papers that a lot of players resented the attention I was paying him, often praising him to reporters. They didn't analyze this and realize that this fulfilled a psychological need for Leon. He didn't have their sense of security.

Also, the other players never did realize the time I spent with him individually. Apart from them. When they didn't even know I was talking to him. Leon came in to me one day and told me, "Let me go home. These guys don't even like me." He said, "I've been poor all my life. I don't need the money that you're paying. You'd be doing me a big favor if you let me go home." Now with a climate like that, what good is it going to do me to fine him for missing a meeting? He wants to go home anyhow. He's just stubborn enough and enough of an individual that he might go. Here's a great talent, probably the greatest a coach is exposed to in a lifetime. Knowing everything I did about him, am I going to push him into something like the Duane Thomas situation in Dallas? Thomas put down the football, that's all. Just quit playing. People said, Well, you know, he'll come to his senses when they put him under the gun. Did he? He just went to San Diego and stood in the end zone for a half hour without moving and then quit playing. Leon told me, "I miss my mother, and the home cooking and I miss the people back home and these people don't like me around here." He said, "Damn this football, I don't need it. Let me go home."

With Leon, I always had two ways to go. The easy way when he had a little temper tantrum or something was just throw the book at him. Just say, "You're suspended. Go home." That would make me a big man with the players or a big man with the press: Geez, here's a guy who has convictions, here's a firm leader type. Maybe I'd have been better off personally if I had done something like that. But I really felt I had a responsibility. If I had it to do over again I'd do it the same way. I'd go as far as I could with the kid, stay with him, help make a football player.

So we went that way through his rookie year. It worked to my satisfaction. He led the East in rushing, even though missing nearly four full games with a slight cartilage tear. I had such a solid relationship with him that at the end of his first year when his contract came up for renewal, even though the N.F.L. was beckoning and his agent could have made a deal, Leon signed with us again. This time for two years. A coup for the C.F.L. Barrow signed him. I'd done the work.

Barrow Called Them High-Priced Losers

I had some pangs in the spring of 1971, even apart from the arrival of John Barrow. It reminded me of that song about "breaking up that old gang of mine." Tom Wilkinson said goodbye without bitterness or surprise when I traded him to B.C. Lions. He'd helped Argos slaughter them 50-7 the previous October. Wilkie had heard from me after our disastrous Calgary game what the Argonaut directors thought of him. He welcomed a chance somewhere else and only hoped he could transfer his off-season job with Canada Life as well. Bob Swift was traded to Winnipeg, looking ahead, not back, like the pro he is. He was attending a teachers' college near Lancaster, Pennsylvania, when he was told. He and his wife spent the first day of his trade teaching his two-year-old daughter Joelle to say "Winnipeg". Don Jonas in Orlando said he felt he still had a chance when Theismann was signed but when Barton signed, too, he knew that any day now he'd be traded. He went to Winnipeg to become one of the dominant figures in Canadian football instantly, because they made the job all his, every minute of it, the situation he felt most comfortable in. I knew how good he could be so I made sure I sent him to the worst team I knew. Ottawa, B.C., and Edmonton wanted him.

I had to let Bobby Taylor and Mike Blum go, for different reasons. Blum was a good, tough football player but he came in to me after the 1970 season and told me that he was working for a brokerage firm and expected to make upwards of $26,000 and had just been told that according to Ontario laws he couldn't stay with this brokerage firm and play football too. His decision was he had to make a lot more money from football. He told me how much. "We can't pay you that kind of money," I told him. He played it right to the hilt. Said, "Look, if I don't get it I'm going to quit."

About that time Ralph Sazio called me from Hamilton and told me Ellison Kelly was available. We could use someone like him for our offensive line. He was getting long in the tooth but is great for a football team, has a great attitude, knowledge, experience, and leadership qualities. I made the trade, glad to do it.

The funny part was that Blum came out after that and said that before I traded him called him in one day and asked if he was in agreement with some of the things Dick Thornton had written in a book (which we'll come to). Blum said he told me, yeah, he certainly was, and as a result I traded him. That was not the way it went at all. But then nothing ever was quite right for Blum. It was either too hot or too cold, or we weren't getting enough to eat or we were eating too much, or we were working too hard, or not enough.

He really carried a deep grudge after his trade. Maybe that's standard. Almost any player traded or cut from a football team feels it wasn't his ability but a personal dislike by the coach that caused his dismissal, and Blum was an extreme example. Blum wouldn't allow himself to admit that he himself had most to do with him leaving the Argos that time. (He returned in 1973.) Also, regarding what he said about me – well, he ran down the Ottawa coaches after he left there, too. Everybody is out of step but Blum.

Bobby Taylor's pride was hurt when I let him go. He also said it was personal. It wasn't. I knew what a great contribution he'd made to the football team. If it had been personal I wouldn't have spent all those years looking the other way in practice so he wouldn't drive me nuts. I traded Bobby Taylor because he hurt his knee in 1970 and when we started work in

1971 he had slowed a step because of the injury. When we went out in pre-season drills in April and May, catching the ball he was just not his old agile, aggressive self. Another factor, not the dominant one, was that Mike Eben was coming back with us on a deal with Edmonton. There was a Gabler-type personality clash between Eben and Taylor. Taylor was openly insulting with Eben every chance he got because Eben was simply not the kind of a guy you often encounter in a locker room full of football players. He was taking his doctorate at the University of Toronto in Germanic Studies – but he'd also been the All-Star flanker in the Western Conference when we loaned him to Edmonton for 1970. His whole element was academic, up until a certain point of each year when the academic in him was overpowered by his desire to play football. What is there about this game that could lure a guy like him? I mean, everything about Eben is consistent right up to the point that he is a football player, which really is against almost everything he stands for. There is great risk involved in football. It is closer to a war situation than any other sport, in sheer physical combat by opposing groups of men. But while it is a very physical encounter, finesse is important too. And that's Eben: quick, a thinker, with great ability to catch the ball.

He'd shown me plenty in his first two years with Argos, 1968 and 1969. But in those years Taylor was at his best and Eben was used mainly for running back punts. In 1970 Edmonton was in trouble at flanker and I'd sent Eben there for what was called future considerations. The future considerations in his case were that he would get the hell back to Toronto after one year. I'd got it on paper. When he was an All-Star, catching 48 passes for 733 yards and five touchdowns (he got another running), Edmonton didn't want to give him up. Coach Ray Jauch came into my office in Toronto to argue, "We can't justify to our fans being so stupid as to take a guy for one year, make a star out of him, then send him back. It is going to hurt us very much."

I modestly mentioned the written agreement I had on this

point with their general manager, Norm Kimball. Jauch didn't know about that. He went back and verified it with Kimball and we didn't hear any more about it. This is an example: regardless of who you are dealing with in football, get it down in black and white. Things can change emotionally. If there'd been any way Edmonton could have destroyed that piece of paper I'm sure they would have. I sympathized. That's all.

I think Taylor realizes now that we showed our appreciation for his years with Argos by the way we handled it when he was cut. We could have taken him to training camp as insurance and cut him late, when it would be harder to catch a job elsewhere. But letting him go early wasn't all unselfishness on our part. Taylor wasn't the kind of guy you wanted in camp unless you were sure he was going to make the team. Because of his outspoken attitude and his temperament, with Taylor there was always a crisis. So we told him to make his own deal. This was the second time he'd had that chance. One earlier year Taylor wanted a big raise and became a little threatening about it. I told him that he had my permission to call anybody he wanted to in the league and look for a job. He made some phone calls and then came back and signed with us. This time he talked to several clubs but signed with Hamilton.

Wilkinson, Swift, Blum, and Taylor – gone. Danny Nykoluk – retired. That pretty well said goodbye to the main members of the old Rogues' Gallery. Except for Dick Thornton. A new bunch of Argos were at the core of things as we got ready for training camp. Theismann and Barton. Corrigall. Leon McQuay. Jim Stillwagon. Paul Desjardins, the center we'd got from Winnipeg for Swift – the trade made mainly because Swift couldn't handle the long snap on third downs or on quick kicks and Desjardins could. We got Zenon Andrusyshyn as kicker. He'd been the golden boy at U.C.L.A. but hadn't been able to make it at Dallas in 1970. Montreal wanted him but we paid him to sit out that year on the coast and come to us in 1971. Gene Mack from Texas was a new linebacker; he'd been a seventh-round draft pick by Minnesota. Larry Brame from

Western Kentucky, who'd been drafted by St. Louis. Mark Ellison from Dayton, a draft choice of New York Giants (he wound up on the New York active roster after we cut him). Counting defensive back Tim Anderson, the N.F.L. first-round draft choice who picked us over San Francisco – Tony Razzano brought him to us in August – we had 17 new faces by the time our team was set. Including Dave Cranmer, who came to us from Calgary in one of those deals that sometimes bring some levity into a coach's life.

Cranmer was a Canadian who always played extremely well against us. Bob Gibson coached him in Bowling Green and knew him well and liked him. He was born in Ontario and wanted to get back there. He told Calgary that he was going to Ontario. They could either trade him or he'd go there to work and give up football. Rogers Lehew, the Calgary general manager, let me know he was available. At the same time Ron Arends, one of our best defensive backs, told me he was retiring. The people he was working for wanted more of his time. I said, "Is there no way you'll change your mind? Go home and think about it." We needed the kid badly. But I knew his style. If he told you no, it was all over.

He said, "You know me, Coach. I've made up my mind. I'm through with football. That's it."

When Cranmer became available, Rogers Lehew said he'd take Arends. It was a great chance to cheat him out of Cranmer. All I had to say was, "Go ahead, Arends is all yours." But I didn't.

I said, "How about taking Ray Langcaster from Xavier University and somebody else?"

"No. I want Arends."

"Now I have to be truthful with you," I said. "Arends is not going to play football. He's going to retire."

Rogers thought that was another one of my ploys. The worst of it was, I knew he'd think that. So it was devious in a way. The more I tried to convince Rogers that Arends was going to retire the more Rogers was sure I was trying to screw him. So I finally gave in. Rogers insisted, you know. Wouldn't take no for an answer.

I called Arends and told him I was trading him to Calgary. He was upset. He was retiring and didn't want to be traded – which would make it look as if we didn't want him any more. I explained the whole situation to him. Told him exactly what had happened. To make it a little less of a steal, we made it Arends and Ray Langcaster. But I knew that it was going to be no more than Cranmer for Langcaster because Arends wasn't going to go, and he didn't.

We had one more rhubarb going into that 1971 camp: Dick Thornton's book. If you could keep Thornton playing and not thinking about anything else, you had something going for you. But he'd always fancied himself as a writer. He'd hooked up with a publisher, Longmans Canada, a year or so earlier and wrote this book that was supposed to be published just before the 1971 season. By some personal connection between an Argo director and a Longmans director, I think, a copy of this book got to Barrow. I know Johnny F. Bassett had a copy of it once. Anyway, parts of it came to me. Some excerpts.

I talked to Thornton. "What the hell are you doing, saying those things about me?"

He said, "Hell, those are compliments!"

Like, he'd written that I was liable to choke under certain circumstances. That kind of compliment I don't need. There was a lot of other stuff about players that I guess he thought had some clang or exposé value for sales.

There was a rumor that Argos somehow had the book stopped. That's not right. Barrow told me that the top man in Longmans read it and decided it wasn't good enough – even though they'd encouraged Thornton to write it and had helped him with it. Not long after the rejection, but before that was made public, Thornton came in to me and said he realized he'd made a mistake with the book and was sorry. You know the look he'd have. All sincerity. He said, "Look, you tell me. If you want me to print the book, I'll print it. If you don't want me to print it, I won't print it."

I said, "Damn you. You already got the word that it won't be printed. So you're giving me a chance to veto it after the fact."

He had some sheepish excuse. When he walked out of the room I had to laugh about him trying to be so cute. Although, of course, he might eventually get another publisher.

None of this should take away from my real regard for Thornton as a football player. On the field he could make the big play, could play quarterback, defensive back, wide receiver, anything.

Always before in training camp he pretty well had it made. He was just that good on defense. Now I thought that the best way to put him in his place, let him know I didn't want any more of this book kind of jazz, was to put on a little pressure. So we put him on offense in camp and told him he had to make the team as a wide receiver. I always had the idea probably he'd wind up back on defense. But to show you the kind of guy he is, what talent he has, he worked so diligently at the wide receiver position that he made the team there. We didn't have anybody better. He played seven games at wide receiver and did well. Then I put him back on defense and he intercepted seven passes just before the season was over to be about third in Canada in interceptions.

That's why a football coach had to like Thornton. And thinking back, he wasn't any harder on me in that book than he used to be on as good a coach as Bud Grant, who was at Winnipeg when Thornton first went there. I'd known Thornton away back when he was at Northwestern and I was at South Carolina. When he was in Toronto, in his first year and we were getting ready to play Winnipeg, he'd take it on himself to write me, usually on pink paper or green paper or something like that, a complete scouting report on Winnipeg. It was always zeroed in on Bud Grant. It was really funny. I wished I had some of that stuff for posterity after Bud Grant went to coach Minnesota Vikings. Thornton bumrapped the hell out of Bud Grant, right down to his Hush Puppies shoes and his coat that didn't fit. His scouting report usually focussed on how in the game Winnipeg would concentrate all their efforts on trying to make Thornton look bad. That was what Winnipeg would spend all their time doing, of course – making Thornton look bad. He had the idea that the whole Winnipeg football team was after him. He'd remind me constantly that Bud Grant would never do anything about adjustments at half time, could never talk to the players, but would just go in the shower room and stay by himself while the players took care of the whole half time atmosphere themselves, and might just go out and win the football game in spite of Bud Grant. He also told about Bud Grant hunting with some players. After they'd been out in the field for several hours he reached in his pocket and brought out a candy bar. And chomped it bit by bit while all the rest of them were starving. Thornton made such a fetish out of telling me how bad Bud Grant was that I knew it was only a matter of time before he got to me. I wasn't very surprised when I read what he said about me in that book. I always felt Grant was a great coach, so why should I worry?

With this varied crew, we started getting ready for the season. For about a month before we went to training camp the quarterbacks and about 28 others worked out daily in a conditioning program. Then, as usual, a week before the mid-June camp we called a special few days of work for the quarterbacks, receivers, linebackers, and defensive backs. They threw the football around and we got a good chance to look at new players and see their running form, their concentration when catching the football, their moves. We knew what they looked like in films but the close-up, first-hand look is better. Also it gave us an opportunity to get an early start on pass patterns and to help bring the quarterbacks' arms around slowly so that in the first couple of days of normal training camp they wouldn't be stiff and sore. It did something the same for running backs, giving them a chance to get to camp with their feet toughened up a little so they wouldn't have to lose training camp time with blisters.

This early indocrination period led us into training camp. This is always something new for players just out of college. A good experience, an identifiable beginning: they pulled into that long driveway at St. Andrews, a boys' school at Aurora north of Toronto, parked their cars and were assigned a room and a roommate. Usually we'd pair guys who play the same position so that they could compare notes and talk. We always had a good training camp feeling. I often get letters from players I had to cut, talking about how much they liked our camp in comparison to others. The coaches felt the same way about it. We had a whole house to ourselves, at the central part of the campus near the dormitories and dining hall. Besides our bedrooms, we had a meeting room with a nice fireplace, big circular table and a blackboard. Adjoining was a little office for when I had to talk contracts or disciplinary problems or anything else in private. There was a sitting room specifically for the press, when they weren't in with the coaches. And another sitting room where parents, girl friends, or other friends of the players could come in and talk to the coaches. We always had an icebox kept full by Al Epstein, a man in his 70s who was retired from everything but the Argos. He'd do anything he could to help the Argos. He didn't want pay and often wouldn't even turn in a bill for keeping the icebox full of beer, martini mixes, manhattan mixes, and so on. He would take our films into the city each night and pick them up the next day. A lovely guy – unless someone he didn't know was trying to get into our dressing room. Then he was a tiger. We called him our unofficial coach.

Everyone in camp ate meals together. The kitchen staff would put out cold cuts and bread and different things to make sandwiches at night when we were working. Same for the players if they were hungry before bed. The players also could go off campus for a beer if they wanted, but we spelled this out in the playbook. The idea was, if you want to have a beer or a drink, you are on your own. No drunkenness. Later in the season anyone caught in a bar for any reason in the 48 hours before a game would be fined. It wasn't a rule we could enforce easily but it was there if necessary. Basically, we told them, you're responsible people and you're going to be held responsible for what you do and say. But we're not going to police you.

I think probably the toughest job in professional football is bringing a bunch of guys to training camp and have them all fire their best shot and then ultimately having to tell many of them that they are not good enough to make the football team. The first year I was in Toronto I felt it was my responsibility to call guys in individually when I cut them and tell them what the reasons were. On the last cut in 1967 this took me five hours and cured me permanently.

I remember one kid from Purdue, a fullback, Gene Donaldson. He played 11 games for Argos in 1966 and was a good football player but we'd used up all our import positions on the team and I couldn't keep him. When I told him he was going to be cut, he just said, "No, you can't cut me."

It was the damnedest situation I ever got into. He sat down in a chair right opposite me and said, "Coach, I'm better than these other guys. I want to play. I'm not going to leave." I didn't know what the hell to do. I spent nearly an hour with him before I could get him out of the office. It almost got to a point where I had to call the police and tell them to dismiss this guy from the football team. I liked the kid but we just couldn't make room for him. Later he played some with the Buffalo Bills.

He was an exceptional case, of course. But when you cut them, very few don't have tears in their eyes, tears of frustration, tears of anger, and certainly tears of sadness. It is a big thing in a kid's life to leave his home and his home town and that makes it even tougher, getting fired. I'm kind of a home town boy myself. Each kid in football has come out of a home town somewhere, or a close-knit community in a larger city. He goes to college and in his senior year if he's good enough for pro he'll have won awards and other honors. He comes back to the home town and is acclaimed as a fine athlete and everyone knows he's going to be playing professional football in the N.F.L., the Canadian Football League, or whatever. They see him working out to get ready. The day he goes they have a party to see him off on his professional career. After all that, it is a tough thing for a kid not to succeed. And to have to go back after a while and say, "Well, I didn't make it." Nobody at that stage of maturity wants to admit to the home town people that he's failed in what he attempted. You can fail at a job as an accountant or something like that and nobody knows about it. You take another job some place else. But when you try to make it as a football player, your home town has sent you there. Periodically your friends have been making calls to ask, How's this kid doing? Is he going to make the team? And when you don't make it, they put it in the home town paper: He's been cut. And everybody knows, who had such high hopes. And the kid has to face them.

The atmosphere changes once they make it, of course. Then the hand is out to get more money, and they're asking, "Can't you do this? Can't you do that?" It was touch and go with Bill Symons his first year, 1967, whether we were going to keep him. He came from B.C., with a bad knee that he got with the Green Bay Packers. We were playing him as a defensive back and slotback, and it boiled down to Symons or somebody else. Symons was pretty sure that he was going to be cut when he walked in to see me. I liked Symons. He was so fresh and original and real. I think that the exposure to so many things that he got later, TV commercials and the Schenley award and so on, hurt him as a football player. But as a fresh country boy with the cowboy boots and the T-shirt and levis and stuff like that at first, he was the kind of a kid you'd want your son to be. Anyway, when he walked in there that day in 1967, expecting the worst, I remember it vividly.

I said, "Do you think you are good enough to make this football team?"

He said, "Yes, sir. I think I am."

I said, "You made it."

The look of relief. He went to the phone and reported to his wife: I'm here! I made the football team! That's the other side of the tough, tough thing, when you call in a kid with so much hope and shatter his hopes.

That first year of such scenes was too much for me. Every year after that in training camp I'd tell the football team early, as I did in 1971, that whatever was done with the football team was my responsibility. "But if you are cut you are going to be cut by your position coach. And when you are cut I don't want to see you. I'm telling you right now that I appreciate the effort you will make, more than you know. But don't think badly of me if I don't shake hands with you and say goodbye."

I also told them it was important to remember that this football league has nine teams. If players went out in the inter-squad and exhibition games and played well, being cut by this football team wouldn't necessarily spell the end of the world. If they'd showed that they were football players somebody in this league would pick them up.

At the time Barrow was hired he had the title but I still had all the responsibilities, hiring and firing. At the beginning of the season he talked to me about coming up to meet the football team. There was another dispute over training camp pay. He asked if he could talk to the football players on that. I said, "I'll go one step further, I'll bring you in and introduce you to the players. You take it from there, have a meeting with them, and I'll leave the room."

Instead of talking solely about averting a strike, he single-handedly achieved near disaster. Whatever else he said, he called them a high-priced bunch of losers and told them they were going to have to have their hair cut or they weren't going to represent the Toronto Argonauts. Great for the harmony I try to achieve in camp. My own position is that while I don't campaign for it, I know a lot of good people with long hair. Any other position today is a little stupid. Mel Profit and Dave

Raimey and a whole bunch of them came to me and were ready to quit football if Barrow was going to have anything to do with our operation. He had an open confrontation with Profit in that meeting. After that, the rest of his association with the 1971 football team was from well in the background.

The main thing in training camp is preparation, both physical and mental – mental being the part Barrow didn't help. We spent the 90-minute morning practice in shoulder pads, helmets, and shorts, mainly for conditioning and teaching. In the afternoon we would put on the battle garments and get into the hitting.

The camp functions, not necessarily in this order, are first to get the coaches familiar with personnel and give them an opportunity to make a choice between holdovers and new players. It's also an indocrination period, to put in new styles of offense and work in new people. It is also a conditioning period. And finally it is a polishing period before the exhibition games which lead into your first league game.

So everything stems from camp: the discipline, the way that you expect players to do things, the grasp they get of your philosophies.

We knew them all pretty well in advance, of course. But only in a statistical way, with new players. We had files on them, college coaches' reports. We'd been to their colleges to look at films. We had taken most of them out individually to dinner to get to know them personally. By the time we brought a man to Toronto to sign him, we'd have a lot of written information on him as a player. But camp tells a lot more. As a great coach, Bud Wilkinson, once said, potential means nothing, performance is what counts. Some guys come in heralded as All-American, all-this and all-that, and don't make it. Another player may have been a bust at college, whose college coach says this guy is a loser, he can't play. But because he's motivated by that dollar bill he turns out to be a great football player. Conversely, some kids who were motivated by the old college try can't stomach the professional atmosphere.

So we eat with the players, observe them under duress, watch them under difficult conditions of heat and exhaustion, to see how they are going to react. You can get a very good indication from camp as to what is going to happen to this man or that when you are on the five-yard line and you have to score. And you stash away other impressions: guys that lose their poise and will fight at the drop of a hat. For a man to show fight in football is good only as long as it doesn't affect the way he plays. He can't get himself so wound up over any one confrontation that it affects the rest of his game. A player fights to assert himself, to protect himself and to show the other guys that they can't do this to him. But we cautioned the guys that once the football season started, if you fight and get thrown out of a game, we will fine you because we can't accommodate somebody who can't control his passions.

After each workout when we came off the practice field all the coaches would go to the meeting room and grab a beer or pop or coffee and sit down with the whole training camp roster. We'd read them through, with each coach commenting on each player. We'd change our coaches around in training camp from position to position so each would watch each player at some time. In going down the list it was invaluable to me to hear opinions, not so much about ability in football but on guys as individuals.

Abofs; they'd comment. Aldridge; they'd comment. Andrusyshyn, Balasiuk, Barrett, Barton, Bland, Brame, Bray. Dye, Eben, Ellison. Hudspeth, Inskeep, Johansen. Markle, Martin, Mathews, McQuay. (Superlatives, along with some head-shaking.) Petmanis, Profit, Raimey. (One day there was a rumor that Profit and Raimey were going to be traded to B.C. and they got some tape reading B.C. and stuck it on their helmets.) Theismann, Thornton, Thorpe, Tomlin. Vijuk (whom we'd got from Winnipeg in the Jonas deal). Wells, West, Williams. Sixty-three names. . . .

. . . "A good kid but he won't hit a snake on the head."

... "I don't read him that way. Lacks experience but I think when the going gets tough he'll hit. Right now he's feeling his way along."

... "A pain in the ass."

... "This guy can do it but if you're not watching him all the time he'll rest."

Twice a day I'd find out what each coach thought of each player as a person and as a football player, and what they thought about his football aptitude. That phrase is a little hard to explain but there is a certain kind of kid who has football aptitude. He can learn his plays. He won't be dropping the ball when he's coming out of the backfield. On a pass he'll catch the ball most of the time. In his take-off from the line of scrimmage, he isn't jumping offside but isn't late either and can read defenses well. So football aptitude is really an intelligence factor that has very little to do with anything but football.

Over a two-week period in training camp, if there was a consistency of good reports on a certain guy we'd want to see how he did in an exhibition game. On some players we'd often refer later to things we'd learned in training camp. I can give an example from the 1971 and 1972 seasons: George Wells. He has all the ability in the world. But in training you would have to watch him and drive him and remind him. It was carried over into his league play. Sometimes he'd come across the line of scrimmage, hurdle three people, one-handedly knock down a pass, intercept a pass, pick up a fumble, or kill a quarterback. And then three or four times he'd sit on the line of scrimmage and wouldn't do anything – look like he wasn't even thinking about the game. We knew that he was that way in camp. When it happened in games too in 1971 and 1972 we warned him, put up with him about as long as we could, then let him go. Later Hamilton picked him up. He looked better there. What it means is he changed his ways. He's not any better a football player than he was in Toronto but he had that two or three weeks when he had to look at himself in the mirror and check his wife and his baby and say, "Christ, I'm out of a job. I'm not going to make that mistake again." So he goes to Hamilton and plays a lot harder. But I don't know if those leopards can change their spots entirely. At times when looking at films in 1972 I saw him go half-hearted again. But he was some better.

RIGHT
My high school coach, Butch Nowak, always called me Louie so I wouldn't get uppity. But when I made All-State he got me out of bed on a Saturday morning to tell me.

Photo—University of Illinois

BOTTOM
I weighed 107 when I started to play–and I always had to hitchhike six miles home after practice. But five years later I was with Illinois in the Rose Bowl. They let me play when we had it won.

Photo—University of Illinois

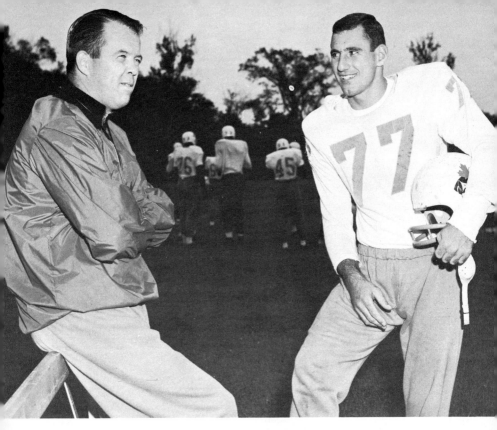

The Rifles brought me to
Toronto–here with Leon
Mavity.

Photo—Graphic Artists

TOP RIGHT
Moving to Argos in 1967, I
had two months to pick a
team–and end five years of
last place finishes.

Photo—Toronto Sun Syndicate

BOTTOM RIGHT
The coaches: Ackerman,
Gibson, Cahill, Rountree,
Johnston: we had trouble
with players and owners,
but never on the coaching
staff.

Photo—Graphic Artists

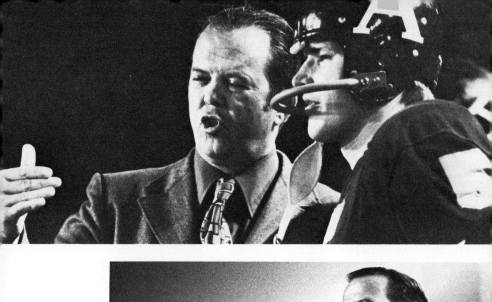

Terry, Christy, Lisa, and
Steve. In 1972 the kids at
school sang Goodbye Cahill
to Christy. Missing are my
wife, Shirley, and our baby,
Betty Lynn. Lisa and Betty
Lynn were born in Canada.
Photo—Toronto Sun

TOP RIGHT
Big day for Argos: Joe
Theismann picks out a
Toronto jersey.
Photo—Toronto Sun Syndicate

BOTTOM RIGHT
Training camp, with
Theismann. Leon McQuay's
agent, Tony Rozzano, walks
behind.
Photo—Terry Hancey

With Mert Prophet, the
trainer, and Jim Rountree.

Tension would keep building
until I hit them with the
"Let's go!" routine and
they'd be out the door.

Photo—Terry Hancey

TOP RIGHT
Dick Thornton, a free spirit.
But on the field, all-pro.
Photo—Terry Hancey

BOTTOM RIGHT
No. 57 is Charlie Bray.
Theismann and Mel Profit in
background. Sidelines,
Toronto.
Photo—Terry Hancey

TOP
Out of town, Argonauts
were the team everybody
loved to hate.
Photo—Terry Hancey

BOTTOM
When you lose, the
reporters come in quietly.
Bill Stephenson, CFRB, and
Jim Hunt, CKEY.
Photo—Terry Hancey

LEFT
Some leave the pre-game
warmup early– they're
going for needles.

Photo—Toronto Sun

BOTTOM LEFT
We made it! Last play in
winning the Eastern title
over Hamilton, 1971.

Photo—Toronto Sun

Before the Grey Cup, with
John Bassett. Later
McQuay slipped, I fell.

Photo—Terry Hancey

TOP RIGHT
Sazio loved me for this one:
signing Eric Allen.

Photo—Graphic Artists

BOTTOM RIGHT
When Theismann broke his
leg in 1972, I could feel the
whole bench lose six inches
in height and 30 pounds in
weight.

Photo—Terry Hancey

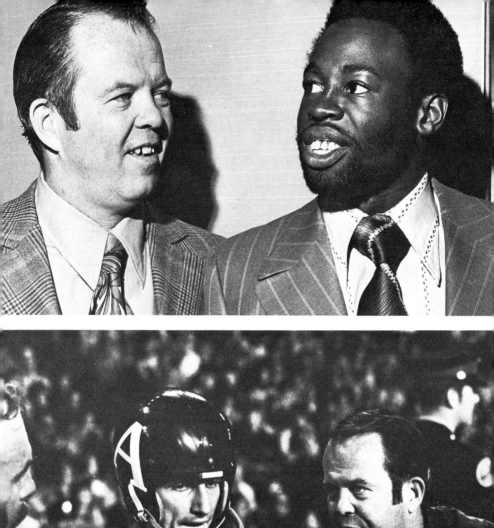

RIGHT
Last game in Hamilton,
1972: the crowd sang
Goodbye Cahill.

Photo—Toronto Sun

BOTTOM
Final score 26-16: I got
that sick feeling that it was
all over.

Photo—Toronto Sun

When McQuay Slipped, I Fell

In 1971 I was named Coach of the Year by the other coaches in Canadian football. Jonas was C.F.L. Player of the Year for Winnipeg. The man I recruited to take his place, Joe Theismann, was Eastern All-Star quarterback and runner-up to Jonas for All-Canadian. Leon McQuay was runner-up to Jonas as Player of the Year. We had six All-Canadians; McQuay as a running back and Mel Profit as tight end, Jim Corrigall at defensive end and Jim Stillwagon at defensive tackle, Marv Luster and Dick Thornton as defensive backs. Besides that, four ex-Argos in Winnipeg were All-Canadians, Jim Thorpe, Bill Frank, Bob swift, and Jonas. Frank, of course, I couldn't take any credit for, but Thorpe and Jonas I'd recruited, and Swift I'd converted to center from fullback. We averaged a paid attendance of 32,845 for 10 games, with all league and playoff games sellouts; that was against an average of 21,254 the year before I arrived in Toronto.

The 10 games we won, to finish first for the first time since 1960, made me the winningest coach in Argonaut history with 43 – three up on Lew Hayman, whose nine seasons ended in 1941. Over the years from 1968 to 1971 I was seventh, in terms of wins, among the 35 pro football head coaches – 26 in the N.F.L. and nine in Canada. Only Eagle Keys was ahead of my record, in Canada. Also in 1971 we won the Eastern championship for the first time in 19 years. Not a bad year but still, on November 28, late in the Grey Cup game there was a little slip, a little fumble. It was to affect my life. Leon McQuay slipped and I fell.

When you look at a season whole, you can see these things. It's laid out all in front of you in a way that shows only the results, doesn't show the really intricate day-by-day decisions caused by injuries, by a player having a nervous breakdown, by finagling to suspend this player or that who was injured but not enough to go on the 30-day list. It doesn't take account of the personal things, like my son, Steve, being badly cut in a game of street football in the summer and my being called away from practice in fear of his life. Or that time during a discussion group in school when my daughter, Christy, was listening to a boy in class say that if Canada was at war with China he wouldn't want to fight but if there was a war with the United States he couldn't wait to start shooting. Including, by inference, Christy Cahill and her parents and the rest of the family.

But then, that is part of being an American in Canada. We hear these caustic remarks people make about the United States: that we're all warmongers, shysters, loudmouths. When it happens to me I don't make it a point to wave the American flag. I'm living in Canada, making my living here, enjoying living here and I like the people here. But I still feel it is my responsibility to defend what I think is right.

So I'll say, "I'm an American."

They say, "Hell, you're different."

They don't know it but they could meet 200,000,000 Americans and not find one like what they *think* an American is like. Funny thing, all my life I lived in the United States. I never heard anyone make a derogatory reference to a Canadian. Never. It was always complimentary. . . .

Just before we came out of camp, I made one change that I regretted but it had to be done. It is very important that a team's trainer get along well with the players. Stan Wilson had been my trainer with the Rifles, a personal friend, very capable. But he was kind of a joker with the players. Sometimes over-familiarity breeds contempt. There were a couple of big men on the football team who didn't like him and started calling him the witch doctor. Pretty soon this spread and other players lost confidence in him. Early in July I had to let Stan go. And I knew that he was a good trainer and a good person. But I was in the position where the whole football team might suffer from this lack of rapport with some players. Mert Prophet had been with us before he went to York University. Mert was admired and respected by us all. When I called him he agreed to come back. It was a simple but painful change, to restore harmony in the dressing room.

By the time we won all four of our exhibition games and our first four league games, we could see exactly what we had in quarterbacks: sooner or later Theismann was going to win over Barton, just as sooner or later Jonas had been going to win over Wilkinson; in both cases on the basis of more natural ability. But Barton had more exposure. Right then Theismann needed a Barton. I'm confident that it takes about five years for a pro quarterback to get the experience he needs to be great. If we'd left Theismann in there all the time he would constantly be rushing in where angels feared to tread. He'd throw the ball regardless of the situation because he has such great confidence in his arm and his ability. When you're at a formative stage, you can't do that playing against professionals. So he needed to be cooled down occasionally. To go to the sidelines, quieten down, then go back in and make the big plays. Barton could get in and stabilize. He didn't make big plays necessarily but was very sound and had a good approach to what he was trying to accomplish. By himself he couldn't have won the overall shot, which was later proved. With Theismann available to go in there and supply the adrenalin, it was a happy marriage.

I made the most of it in a way that at the time was unheard of in football: I alternated them on every sequence of plays. If Theismann got a drive started that went 60 yards to a touchdown, Barton would still be at quarterback the next time we got the ball. And Theismann learned as fast as he does everything else. In the first couple of games he had one of the worst pass completion averages in the league, 21 for 48 tries, but by the fifth game he'd risen to better than a .500 average and never looked back. Barton was steadier but never as spectacular.

It's difficult for me to reproduce in words the emotions we felt before each game; each man meeting it differently – the sleepless, the jumpy, the exploders, the deceptively calm. The headlines would be: "Can Argos run win streak to five? Lineups snap up tickets in 30 minutes." Or whatever. The coaches' ritual was to get to the Seaway Hotel several hours before a game, about noon for night games. The first face we'd see was Eppie's, the guy at training camp I mentioned who was our unofficial coach and official friend, general arranger of things. We'd have a bite, play gin rummy, and I'd take a little nap. Eppie would always come in and wake me up and we'd go down to the pre-game meal which was at 4 p.m. for a night game or 10 a.m. for a day game. For the meal, there was a great inclination among our players to get away from steaks and into other things. This was disrupting, especially for John Barrow who had to do the counting. But some players wanted pancakes, some eggs, some steak, some fruit. Some wanted nothing. Eben wanted seafood all the time.

While most of us ate, Mert Prophet, in an adjacent room, started the preliminary taping of ankles and things that take extra time, to get that out of the way. After the meal came the meeting. At the blackboard I went over some detail stuff on the team we were playing and what we'd been working on all week, our own game plan. Rountree or Ackerman went over our defense. These last-minute preparations usually concentrated on new things that we'd put in that week, or opposition formations that were a bit different – a little extra refresher before the game. When this was completed we usually had a couple of hours before we went to the stadium. Eppie would get some room keys and most players would go and lay around the rooms. So would the coaches. I'd play some gin with Eppie, to relax. Some players would want to get down to the stadium immediately and they'd leave.

166

I'd always drive down with Eppie. I'd drive – I'm told very fast – along the Lakeshore to the stadium's back gate and invariably have trouble with the cop. I'd never have my pass. I'd have to identify myself. Eppie would be furious, jumping: "Don't you know who this is? This is the coach! You can't stop him today!" We went through that every week. I'd go downstairs under the stands and walk in and say hello to the players. They'd be dressing. I'd walk in to the trainer's room and see if anybody was going to be shot up before the game with novocaine and listen to any last minute stuff that Mert wanted to tell me. But the shots wouldn't be given at that time. If a guy said that he was having pain, a lot of times he'd change his mind if you said, "Well, we'll give it a little shot." Most players would take the shot rather than real pain but some would rather suffer the pain. The player would go into the pre-game workout and warm up with the aggravation, whatever it was. If a guy still wanted a shot he'd leave the field just before the rest of the team and get it as close to the game as possible so it wouldn't wear off. When you see players leave the warmup early, they're the ones that are going to get nailed with needles.

In the final pre-game talk I pretty well always did the same thing. At home it was the this-is-our-field-and-we're-not-going-to-let-them-take-it-away-from-us routine. I invariably said this was going to be a tough game but some place in the third quarter we were going to take it over for keeps. This was part of the always positive approach. I always cautioned them, "No matter what happens early in the game, don't lose your poise. There is nobody on this football team that can't run 100 yards in 15 seconds. If you can run 100 yards in 15 seconds, which makes you pretty slow really, you can score four touchdowns in a minute. In a football game you should be able to score something like 240 touchdowns. So if you get behind one touchdown, don't think it is the end of the world."

Then there were specifics. Some teams might try something special early in the game. We'd play zone defense on the first couple of plays, feel them out. In the last couple of minutes, when everybody was ready to go on the field, I'd say, "Okay, everybody take a minute to himself." Most of them bent their heads, or went to one knee, to say a silent prayer. I always went out of the room at that time to be by myself. I came back in just as they were getting up off the knee, to say a couple of final words. The first team I had with the Argonauts, probably the best locker room speech I could have given to get them busting the door down was, "The last 12 guys in the room are going to have to play." But now there'd be that lull after the prayer and then Charlie Bray, sitting there, would start with, "All right, all right. Let's go, let's go!" Somebody else back in the room would be saying something. Tony Moro would always be saying something. It would keep building until I hit them with the "Let's go!" routine and they'd be out the door.

We always got together on the sidelines before a game. I'd maybe yell, "One for all and all for one!" Everyone would yell with me, a release of nervous energy. Then they ran into position or to the bench. In the long wait while they played the national anthem, all kinds of things went through my head. The more important the game the longer the anthem seemed to take.

By that time Gord Ackerman and Blackie Johnston were making their way to the spotter's booth on the roof of the stands. They were connected with the bench by phone. The first year I was with Argos I used to wear the headset myself. I broke the cord and almost broke my neck about eight times that season because I'd be doing something and forget I had that son-of-a-bitch on. After that Gibson always wore it and communicated with them. Gordie is a great screamer, you know, and Blackie a great blasphemer. I never thought that I could really think clearly with these guys yelling my ear. But they certainly served a purpose up there. So Gibson had to take the brunt. He relayed to me anything going on that was substantial and worthwhile, for immediate action. A lot of times when they saw something and I was thinking about something maybe two plays in advance and they wanted to get a message to the quarterbacks, they talked right to the quarterbacks. If it meant a change in what we were doing I still had the final decision. Normally, all I carried on the field was a few reminders. I wrote down certain key plays we planned to use. I checked them every once in a while and if we hadn't employed them throughout the game it was a reminder. I often sent in plays from the sidelines. They were intuition plays. I watched the defense myself and heard what the spotters' interpretations of the defenses were and called a play when I thought there was something we could exploit.

Meanwhile on the bench Jimmy Rountree was pretty much in charge of the defensive team. In the first couple of years I called most of the defenses myself but when Rountree matured he turned out to be an excellent field coach, able to size something up in a hurry and make a decision on it and do some teaching right on the field. This was his forte. He did it well.

Also Gibson and Rountree had to make sure we always had enough people on the special teams, for kicking and receiving. It was the responsibility of any player, if he got hurt, to notify the coach that he couldn't play and also whether he was on any special teams that might be required several plays later. Making replacements for injuries during a game is complicated in Canadian football, where you can dress only 32 players really for 24 positions on offense and defense. In the National Football League you've got a backup man for everybody. But with us, if somebody went down we might have to take an offensive guard and make him a defensive end. Right away, there might be a chain reaction of other switches, including finding somebody to take his place on any special team he was on. It's touchy. That's why you see a lot of times 11 men instead of 12 on special teams – a guy's been injured and hasn't notified anybody. It is almost impossible with 32 people and all that is happening to see a special team run on the field and know which one isn't there. We worked on special team assembly every day. Like, Luster would be on the kicking team and we'd say, "Okay, everybody around Luster!" Luster would stand in the middle and they'd kind of jog around him in the circle and we'd count so that everybody knew what his responsibilities were.

Blackie and Gordie came down from the roof a couple of minutes before half time. In the dressing room they went to the blackboard. Their responsibilities were to categorize the opposition offense and defense in terms of tendencies that we'd been assuming all week we'd have to face. They either verified that our assumptions were accurate or outlined changes they'd seen. They hadn't time to do this on the phone but at the half would have it all written down: like, first and 10 on the 20-yard line, this is what they did. And so on. Set down the pattern.

The first thing I did when I walked in at half time was see who was hurt. They'd have gone right to the training room with Mert a couple of minutes before the end of the half. There were usually three or four guys, never more than that. If somebody was hurt seriously they'd be in street clothes, done for the day. The doctors had a consultation area at one side. If a guy had been hit on the head the doctor would be checking his reflexes, looking at his eyes and so on. Maybe he'd say, "Coach, I don't think you ought to play him in the second half." I might say, "Son-of-a-bitch," or something like that but always went along with the doctor. There was no way I was going to be put in a position of saying, "Well, goddamnit, doc, he's going to play," and have him die on the field.

When I got into the main room the two spotters gave me their report and we talked it over. Then I called for the quarterbacks and told them what the situation was and how we were going to combat it. Gibson always stayed with me. Meantime Blackie went to a blackboard in the film room with just the offensive linemen. Gordie had others in a second room, Rountree the defensive backs. Anyone else that wasn't involved might be going to the bathroom, taking a shot, having a cigarette. Then in the last couple of minutes I got on the blackboard and put the changes down so that everybody could absorb them together.

If there was anything drastic, something that we'd been having a lot of trouble with, Rountree or Gordie would get up and go over the thing defensively on the board. Then we'd be ready for the second half. Or as ready as we could get.

I guess I've sometimes given the impression that whenever it's a battle of wits with another club, I've won. Not always, really. But I did win another just before the 1971 season. Zenon Andrusyshyn had a leg injury that let him punt okay but hampered him badly on field goals because of the different leg movement – a sideways swing instead of the straight-through motion of the punt. At the time, a kid named Ivan MacMillan, who was only 19, had been cut by Ottawa. He'd done well at field goals and converts the year before but that was all he could do. Ottawa had found a good kicker, Gerry Organ, who could also play another position. Still, Ottawa didn't want to let young MacMillan go permanently. He was too good. They were trying to make a deal for him somewhere else, partly to keep him available for the future, and partly to keep him away from me. I tried to call him but couldn't find him. Then I called Jack Koffman, the Ottawa sports editor, and asked him where the kid was. He said, "I'll find him and have him call you."

I got Ivan on a plane to Toronto. My first look at him made me think of that expression about a guy being so small he had to step on two bricks to kick a duck in the ass. He was really a little bow-legged kid but he was excited about the prospect of playing in Toronto and wanted to prove a point with Ottawa. I took him to dinner at Carman's Steak House and was real caustic with him. At his size and age, I wanted to put real heat on him and see what he was made of.

The next day at practice he was really nervous. His first two or three kicks from the 20-yard line were just sprayed one way or the other. I was standing right behind him and I said, "Ivan, you're going to kick five from here, and four of them are going to go in, or you're going to be home for supper tonight in that little town you live in up near Ottawa."

He looked as if he was going to die right on the spot. But he kicked all five of them. Then he jumped up in the air with that enthusiastic jump that he always did after every good one in games later. So I told him all right, we'll take a long look at you in practice. I really led that kid on, put a lot of pressure on him, because he seemed like such a boy, such a skinny little kid. I thought if I could put pressure on and he could still kick he had some substance to him. He answered every challenge. Every time in practice, and throughout the season and even into the next season, when he'd miss one and look at me out of the corner of his eye, I'd say, "Ivan, how far is it to your home town?"

Our fourth game was very tight with Ottawa. That's the one he really gloried in. Just about jumped his own height when he kicked three field goals against them and we beat them 30-28. On the season, he was 12 for 20 on field goals and 26 for 30 on converts.

But there was another deal in 1971 that I lost out on. Or was done out of it by Winnipeg being just a little sneakier than I was. A good running back, Ed Williams, had been a star at West Virginia, but decided to drop out before his senior year. He was so close to making our club that I wanted to keep him around, although there was no immediate room on our roster. Winnipeg was interested in him. Earl Lunsford, their general manager, called and asked several times if he could have Williams. I told him no way, that Williams was our guy. However, at that time we had to drop a few people. One I hated to lose was Paul Markle, a young Canadian tight end. He was one of the last guys I wanted to cut and when I did I made this deal with Earl Lunsford: "We'll give you Paul Markle, who'll be a regular for you and a good one. In return, when we put Williams on waivers, you pass on him." He agreed. At the same time Eagle Keys in B.C. wanted one of our players. I told him the same thing: "You can have him if you pass on Williams." They knew what I was trying to do: put him on waivers, have everyone pass on him, then make a deal to pay him not to play for anybody else that year. I'd get him to sign a piece of paper to that effect, then sign him to a contract for the following year. In court it might be binding but we wouldn't have taken it to court because it was actually illegal as far as the Canadian Football League was concerned. So it wouldn't have been worth the paper it was written on, if anybody had challenged it. We did that with several guys. With Williams, we wanted him enough that it wasn't a cut-rate deal; we agreed to pay him his whole contract, just as if he was playing.

So we put Williams on waivers and all teams passed on him and we made this private deal – but at the time it was only verbal. Barrow was supposed to get him to sign, but didn't. Winnipeg came to town. Jim Thorpe, whom we'd just traded, knew Williams and got him over to their hotel. Lunsford talked to him and gave him the jazz about coming out there right away and starting to play. No player likes to sit around doing nothing. They had a couple of drinks and then Lunsford spirited him out of town and onto a plane in the middle of the night. I'd given Markle to Lunsford strictly on the basis that he would leave Williams alone. So he didn't pick him up on waivers but sneaked in behind us and got him anyway.

Come to think of it, I had a little more trouble than usual with ploys that year. The next one came up late in August. We were unbeaten then. We'd won all four exhibition games and then the first four in our schedule – although there's something interesting there, too; that they were so close. Beat Winnipeg 21-20, Saskatchewan 22-17, were a little easier with Montreal 26-14, and then were close again with Ottawa, 30-28. Three games we'd won by a total of eight points. In a good year you win the close ones; in a bad year, you lose them – yet it may be not all that different a football team. A coach knows he isn't any more a genuis to win by two points than he is a deadbeat to lose by two.

Anyway, we had a date in Vancouver August 29. Ed Harrington had a swelling in his thigh and couldn't bend his knee all the way. We felt it was just a temporary thing. As usual, we didn't like to put him on the injured list. Harrington meant too much to our club to lose for a month if we didn't have to.

So we had one of those conversations, much like the thing

with Jim Thorpe the year before. I called Harrington in and said, "How does the leg feel? Are you going to be able to play in Vancouver?"

He said, "Coach, it really doesn't feel like I'm going to be able to play. I think I would jeopardize my career if I played on it." He took a very strong stand against playing.

I immediately recognized a position we could take advantage of. I said, "Well, we think you can play and if you won't we'll have to suspend you." No animosity. Pure business. I called the commissioner's office and said, "We want Harrington to play and he won't go." Ed verified this with Greg Fulton in the commissioner's office. We played in B.C. and lost it 27-24 but the commissioner's office wasn't so trusting any more. They drew up an affidavit covering the matter and insisted that Ed sign it. He did.

I think what happened was we'd made this suspension dodge so valuable that other teams in the league decided to use it, too. Ottawa suspended Dennis Duncan for something or other to keep him off the injury list; Montreal suspended Moses Denson for refusing medical treatment and suspended Bill Massey, for goshsake, for failing to report an injury he'd suffered two years before! They were ruining our good idea. The next time Montreal suspended somebody, incidentally, the commissioner insisted on an affidavit there, too. The player refused to sign it. There must have been something phony about that incident.

A couple of days later after the B.C. game we were being beaten with just a couple of minutes to go in Edmonton when Dave Raimey intercepted a pass. Theismann moved us down with passes until Mike Eben caught one in the end zone and we won 16-15. That was rubbing it in a bit with the Edmonton fans, who were still grumbling about losing Eben. But in our next game in Hamilton Bobby Taylor, Blum, and a few other Argo castoffs played strong football against us and won 30-17. I had one minor satisfaction; I outwitted Taylor on a sleeper play. He was good at these. Had all kinds of dodges. One time years before, with us, he was coming off the field and just fell down on the sidelines inside the white marker. I thought he'd had a heart attack or something. But he'd worked it out with Wilkinson, a sleeper play. That day nobody but I saw him until Wilkie threw him the ball.

Also, one time with us in Ottawa he screened one so well that I thought we were a man short on the field and sent somebody on fast. So instead of Wilkinson and Taylor working the sleeper, we got a penalty for too many men on the field. Taylor was pretty scathing about that.

But in this Hamilton game I turned the tables on him. All of a sudden with Hamilton in the huddle I noticed Taylor on the sidelines. He was just standing there innocently with his helmet off, dangling it from his hand as if he'd been replaced. But he was on the field. I quickly checked their huddle. They only had 11 guys. I started screaming, "Sleeper play! Sleeper play!" but our guys on the field couldn't hear me. Corrigall was right beside me. I grabbed him and told him to get on the field. There was no time to explain. He was looking back at me as much as to say, "Who do I go in for? What do I do?" But my idea worked. The referee saw him coming on late and blew the whistle. The Hamilton play had started and Taylor got the pass and made a good run to around the five-yard line but it was called back and we got a penalty for having 13 men on the field. Taylor almost exploded he was so mad.

We didn't let them savor that win too long. Six days later we had them back in Toronto and beat them 23-14, giving us a first place edge of four points over Montreal, with Hamilton another two points back in third.

As we went on from there in that beautiful football season to win our next four games in a row, I guess I also won first place on the hate-list of football fans outside of Toronto. There was this automatic hate for Toronto, anyway, in most cities. The Hogtown thing reaches from coast to coast, but finally we had the kind of football team that could make them take it and like it. Some nights Theismann was just outright miraculous.

Corrigall, Stillwagon, Harrington, and the first-round N.F.L. draft pick we'd signed, Tim Anderson, were massacring offenses along the way. The columnists talked about our All-Stars, our bankroll, our arrogance. But everywhere we went we drew the biggest crowds; and, besides getting on the football team, the fans loved to get on me.

I think that the main idea people from the stands got was that I couldn't possibly keep any kind of good judgement when I was screaming and ranting on the sidelines. The truth is, a coach must do all those things, involved 100 per cent, without letting it interfere with his thinking processes. In fact, most of what I did on the sidelines was calculated toward certain specific ends.

There were times with Billy Joe Booth or Angelo Mosca or Billy Ray Locklin, where I'd yell and scream at the guy because of something he did well physically. A lot of people would say, "When this guy plays Toronto, Cahill gets him so mad that he plays like hell. It's a disadvantage to Toronto." I don't believe that. If I get the other team worried about Cahill, worried about fighting with me on the sidelines, looking over at me all the time, their attention is divided. They forget what they're doing out on the field. That means they're not doing as good a job at it. So I purposely bait people as much as possible. Also, if anybody yells at one guy enough, an official has to start thinking, "This son-of-a-bitch can't be yelling that much unless there is something wrong, unless he is completely crazy." So instead of yelling just once, if you yell every time somewhere along the line he's going to drop the flag.

Same in yelling directly at officials. You won't find one so responsive that whenever anything flagrant happens and you say, "Hey, did you see that?" that he's going to change his mind. But if you yell at him every time, "They're holding us! They're holding us!", sooner or later in self-defense he's going to take a look. And anytime an official looks he's going to have to call holding, there's so much of it.

So, hell, I'm screaming, "Holding!" and "Offside!" and

"Watch the line-ups!" and all this kind of thing constantly at the officials. The only risk, of course, is that if you yell at him too much he might get mad at you. There's no way in the world that any official goes into a football game with the idea that he's going to beat me because I'm Cahill and he doesn't like me. But if I egg him on too much maybe he'll start looking for things that he normally wouldn't be looking for. Say, "To hell with that son-of-a-bitch!" and maybe call a couple against me. Especially holding, because it's always there.

During a game isn't the only time you can psych opposing players, of course. I used to make a point of going to mid-field and watching the other team during pre-game warmups. I did that first because there would be certain players that I wanted to know more about; Canadians or Americans maybe new to me that I wanted to look at. Also, frankly, it was another way to defy the other team's coach and players; taking not only our end of the field but infringing a bit on their end too. They disliked this. That would start them getting a little upset and thinking about me instead of the game. Except Russ Jackson, before he retired; I never seemed to get to him. He'd be standing there with me a few yards away and he would just put that ball right on the money, with Margene Adkins in full flight. Or drop back and hit one down the middle 50 yards to Vic Washington or Whit Tucker or Ron Stewart. At the same time I'd be close to their kickers and punt returners. I'd always try to get to those guys that were kicking. I'd say, "You son-of-a-bitch, you're not going to come close today." I remember Don Sutherin once before an Ottawa game. He was kicking field goals. I said, "Sutherin, you haven't got the guts to kick it under pressure! You look real good before the game but you're chicken-shit!"

He turned and kind of laughed but it was bothering him. So he'd kick a bad one and I'd cough loudly. The last play of one game, he had a chance to beat us with a field goal from the 42. He stepped up and just kicked that thing right through, like it's got eyes. Last play of the game! Boy, I gave him a lot of pleasure. He looked over at me on the bench and he was laughing. Giardino, or one of those guys from Ottawa, in the off season said to one of our players, "Is that Cahill really crazy? Do you know what he said to me?" But that was where I liked to be before a game, standing in the middle of the field, talking to them.

We went to Ottawa on September 19 and beat them 26-17, giving us seven wins against two losses. Back home on the 25th we beat Calgary 18-7 and that's when Leon McQuay got the torn ligament. Until then in nine games he'd carried 122 times for 938 yards – nearly 500 yards better than the East's second-best rusher, and 213 yards better than Jim Evenson of B.C., who was tops in the West. He carried only five times in the Calgary game and that injury kept him out until the last game of the season, when he still wasn't right. After averaging more than 100 yards a game for nine games, that bad leg had to happen to him and keep him from rushing well over 1,000 yards in his rookie season. Still, we beat Ottawa 12-3 in our next game, without Leon. Being eight points up by then on Hamilton and Montreal, we only had to win one more game to clinch first place. We did it 32-5 in Montreal, and when I walked into the Playback Club at the Westminster Hotel the following Wednesday with a 10 and 2 record, I got a standing ovation. I remembered another time I walked in there, after losing. Shirley was pregnant then with our Betty Lynn. The fans send up questions, you know. One of the questions that day, after the loss, was: "I hear your wife is pregnant. Do you think the baby is going to be as dumb as the father?" Some fans are very lovable people.

We were in bad shape physically after clinching first place. Montreal beat us 28-7 in Toronto. John Trainor, Ed Harrington, and Leon McQuay were all injured. Greg Barton broke a finger in Ottawa. Mike Eben got a bruised lung in the Montreal game.

Right at that point the word came out that the votes of the C.F.L. coaches had been counted and I was named Coach of the Year. I was invited to go to Edmonton and accept it. With the team's injury problems, I didn't want to take even a day off.

When Barrow heard that he came down and volunteered to accept it in my place. I was glad to say okay. It seemed to me a good thing for club harmony. The stories everyone had heard about Cahill and Barrow having problems wouldn't have much credibility if he went out and accepted the Coach of the Year trophy on my behalf. At the same time it was a smart thing for Barrow to do. At that stage my stock was high.

So he went and I stayed home to try to patch up our injured lineup. Our lines had so many injuries that one writer suggested we might activate John Barrow. Knowing the way some of the players felt about him, Rex MacLeod wrote that it would make our practices more interesting, if nothing else. But I couldn't laugh. I was thinking ahead to the playoffs and the Grey Cup and I knew I had to have some help. There just wasn't any around. Then I thought of Danny Nykoluk. He'd been in the hospital the year before with a back injury and complications from a broken rib. He'd retired at the end of the 1970 season and had been honored on Danny Nykoluk day with a lot of gifts, because of his 15 years with Argos. He was always a complete football player as far as we were concerned. What happened to him happens to all football players. He'd got a step slower and a little bit older but he always had concentration and great dedication to the game.

Something Nykoluk never had done in all his tenure was to go to the Grey Cup. It had always been his ambition. And he was what we needed, an offensive tackle. Our offensive line was in bad shape.

I said to the coaches, "I'm going to get Nykoluk." They all said, "There's no way he'll play."

"Well, you just listen to this conversation." I called Nykoluk and said, "Danny?"

"Yeah, Coach. How're you doing?"

"You know what I'm calling for."

"Yeah, I think I do."

"What do you say?"

"What time do you want me there?"

That's how the conversation went. He came back for the last game of the season, when Hamilton beat us 23-15. He was just a shadow of what he'd been, but he helped. Against Hamilton in the two-game Eastern final we took them 23-8 in the first game. A few days later one of the Playback Club's organizers, Ron Barbaro, had some metal tapes made to stick on every player's helmet. They read: "The season ends on November 28. Be there." We had a little picture of the Grey Cup stuck up in every locker. We played a fierce second game with Hamilton. It was a tie, 17-17, giving us the round, 40-25. Somebody asked me after the game if I'd been scared. Scared? I'd been remembering the 1968 and 1969 finals when we took leads into Ottawa, and blew them.

The night before our second Hamilton game I had a dream. I was watching television. Pat Marsden, the CFTO sports commentator, came on and looked right at me and said, "Ladies and gentlemen, you won't believe this, but Argos blew it again." It turned out he was just a little premature.

A few days later we flew to Vancouver. I don't have to tell anybody what the Grey Cup means in Canada. It's the Super Bowl, Kentucky Derby, Mardi Gras, and the rock festival at Woodstock all rolled into one. For the fans, it's one long party. For new football players in Canada, it's something they can't believe until they see it and feel it: a whole nation split, East against West. For players and coaches who have been around it all their lives it is still the most tension-filled game of the season. I'd been waiting for that moment for 11 years, since I landed in Montreal.

Calgary manhandled us in the first quarter. Held us to one first down. Dropped Theismann for losses a couple of times. And they scored a touchdown after one 53-yard march.

Early in the second quarter Mel Profit picked off Theismann's sideline pass and went 55 yards to the Calgary 11, but then a pass to Profit (too high) and another to McQuay in the end zone went bad and MacMillan kicked a field goal. Tim Anderson stopped one Calgary drive with an interception. Calgary got the ball back when Theismann fumbled on their side of the mid-field. Their big play after that was Jerry Keeling's 40-yard pass to Rudy Linterman on our five. Corrigall threw the next play for a loss but then Jesse Mims went over center on a draw play to score.

I tried Greg Barton at quarterback late in the second quarter but it was still Calgary 14, Toronto 3, early in the third when we got our one break of the game. Andrusyshyn's punt was fumbled on the Calgary 36 by Jim Sillye. Joe Vijuk picked it up and lateraled to Roger Scales, who went in to score. MacMillan converted, making it 14-10.

We made only two first downs in the third quarter, Calgary one; which means defense was dominating the game. MacMillan missed his second long field goal of the day but it went for a single point, 14-11.

In the fourth quarter it was even tighter. We got one first down, Calgary none. There'd been a total of 18 first downs in the first half; the total was four in the second. But we were picking up five yards or so on every exchange of kicks, Andrusyshyn averaging that much better than their Jim Furlong. I paced the sidelines. Tried Barton again. Replayed in my mind that good early long gainer to Profit, thinking if we'd only got a touchdown there instead of a field goal we'd be up instead of down. The team was playing it tough, giving up nothing – but we had to get one break. If we could get close enough to tie with a field goal, I was confident we could win it on punts if there was no other way.

Then we got the break. Typically, it came from my old buddy the author, Dick Thornton. We had Calgary back on its own 30, second down. Keeling dropped back and threw long for Jon Henderson. Thornton intercepted on our 45. Our blockers picked him up instantly and started clearing the way. Thornton made some fine moves. The blockers got to everyone but Keeling himself, who dropped Thornton on the Calgary 11.

There were still minutes left to play. The field goal was there but would only tie. Even though I was confident we could win in either regular time or overtime, we also had at least two plays to try for the winning touchdown right now. Theismann was at quarterback. He sent McQuay to the right side on a pitchout. Dick Suderman got him at the hash-marks after a four-yard gain. The next play was to McQuay again, a sweep around the left end. The tartan turf had been sponged off before the game but there had been more drizzle and it was slippery. McQuay slipped. When he went down one defensive back, Larry Robinson, hit him. The ball popped out of his hands. Another defensive back, Frank Andruski, fell on it. The chance, even for the field goal, was gone.

We weren't dead yet. It took the next misplay to kill us finally. Our defense held them on two plays. Furlong's punt went to the Toronto 48. Harry Abofs, in pursuing it, kicked it out of bounds. If he had fumbled it out of bounds or it had gone out of bounds in any other way, it would have been our ball with about six plays left to get in close again. But when Abofs kicked it out of bounds that meant Calgary was given the ball. We held them. They kicked and we got the ball back on our own 28 but there was time for only one play and it wasn't enough. We won 13-8 on first downs, out-gained them 258 yards to 214, outpassed them, out-kicked them – and out-fumbled them. That last was the pregnant statistic. With a win I could have gone back to Toronto with some security. Which is what I meant earlier when I said that when McQuay slipped, I fell.

Beating Baltimore to The Flea

A few weeks after we returned from the Grey Cup the directors called me in to talk contract. I had one more year to go in the four-year deal I'd signed early in 1969. I thought if I was in the National Football League and in a five-year period went from last place and put together a Super Bowl team, hell, the sky would be the limit. I'd have a job for life. In my own mind my big decision was going to be whether I would sign a long term contract and cast my lot with the Canadian Football League forever, or think about going to the National Football League. I was thinking about that when I walked in.

What they offered was a one-year extension on my old contract. You know, the hay was in the barn, everything had been accomplished except winning the Grey Cup. The season ticket sale was getting close to the park's capacity. After five years before 1967 of not being in the playoffs we'd built a tradition of winning. Went to the Grey Cup for the first time in 19 years. Had the first Schenley Award winner. Had the first Coach of the Year. Recruited some of the best football players in the history of the game. Were the most looked at team in the history of the league. In wins over four years I ranked seventh among the 35 pro head coaches in North America. These were all not figments of my imagination but facts. And they offered me a one-year extension. It was a strange, strange thing.

I guess as long as adrenalin flows, owners and directors are all going to be fans first, analysts later. A couple of them at the meeting did say, "Well, let's look at what he's done." And they found out what the record was. But they had to sit down and have a meeting to realize it. They'd been playing it a game at a time and, like in a television program or anything else, all they were remembering was the last highlight. The loss in the Grey Cup.

I went home from that meeting and told my wife, "There is no way these people really want me around."

Then the newspapers began to ask, "Why not give Cahill the contract he deserves?" That's what I thought, too. In the next meeting I walked into Bassett's office, with Lew Hayman there as well, and asked for a four-year contract. By then they were offering me three.

Lew said, "Leo, this is the longest contract an Argonaut coach has ever got – three years."

I said, "Hell, Lew, I've been on a four-year contract." So they looked it up. Until then Bassett and Lew and all the others didn't even realize that I had been on a four-year contract. Still Bassett said, "This is what I'm prepared to offer you: a three-year contract for $28,000 a year."

I continued to argue for four years.

"Listen," he said, "this thing has reached a bad point. Now, if I were you I probably wouldn't sign. I'd probably hold out and be bullheaded. That's the way you and I are. We are a lot alike in a lot of things. But you'd be doing me a personal favor if you'd sign this contract and get this thing over with."

Charlie Dubin had drawn it up after our earlier discussions. I read it. The contract spelled out a division of authority that hadn't been in my old one. Barrow would be in charge of the negotiation list, hiring the trainer and other people. I thought about it. And I made the decision. With a three-year contract, Barrow was not going to be able to run me out. Therefore I could justify making concessions. We'd get along. Common sense would prevail. It seemed to me that neither one of us had won the war. We were going to have to live together for three years. Two adults should be able to accomplish what was best for both and the team. Bassett, urging me to sign the contract, said he wanted me to know that I'd be with the football team as long as he was.

"You're my style of guy," he said. "More than the other guy. I've got big plans for you with this organization." Those were his words. I picked up the pen and said, "Make it thirty." Meaning $30,000. I couldn't stand being paid less than Barrow. Bassett said okay. I signed, and walked out of there thinking of how I could patch here, patch there, and get back into the Grey Cup again. This time, I was sure we'd win it. I went farther than that. I thought, if I'm around here for 20 years I'll win them five or six Grey Cups.

I started right then to do the things that should be done. Leon McQuay helped me in two early new-player signings. Two of his friends still with eligibility left at the University of Tampa were Ron Mikolajczyk and Noah Jackson, both of them offensive linemen, where we'd had a gaping hole in our Grey Cup team that Nykoluk, for all his trying, hadn't been able to fill. Mikolajczyk had been a Little All-American. He was 21, Jackson near that, when I signed them. Mikolajczyk was six-four, 266 pounds; Jackson six-two, 263.

Tampa was furious, of course. Again. First they lost McQuay, and then two top linemen. Milt Dunnell wrote a column in the *Star* from Tampa reporting that no Canadian Football League scout would be allowed on the Tampa campus in future and that if I appeared in person "there might be a public hanging beneath the stately eucalyptus trees." This was because we had done what the N.F.L. wouldn't do – signing players before they graduated. If a college said, "We're damn mad because he wrecked our football team," I'd agree they had a point. But I repeat that there's nothing to prevent a player from finishing college in style in the off-season, when he's making a good salary from football.

To me, signing those two was the only good thing that happened that winter. March was one of the worst months of my life, personally. My father had a heart attack. Early in the month he became seriously ill. I went home and spent most of two weeks at his bedside, with my mother. When he died the sense of loss I felt, and still feel, was one of the strongest emotions I've ever had to cope with.

The only solace was to get back to work, hard, to rebuild the team to do the job we hadn't quite done in 1971. And then I had a little luck.

Eric Allen was one of the finest players in the history of Michigan State. He was on Hamilton's negotiation list. We'd known about him for a couple of years but had been put off a little by his size – only 162 pounds. They called him The Flea. Al Dorow, the Hamilton coach in 1971, had come from Michigan State and had no such reservations. So we'd missed him. Then in his senior year he'd won the Chicago *Tribune*'s Silver Football award as the outstanding player in the Big Ten. He was the leading ground gainer in Michigan State history and had set several fantastic single game records. Baltimore drafted him fourth, which meant they really wanted him.

Meanwhile, Hamilton had fired Al Dorow and hired Jerry Williams, who'd been head coach at Philadelphia. And in the spring Ralph Sazio, the Hamilton general manager, went to Europe on a trip. Jim Rountree, who was working the Big Ten for us, found out that Hamilton hadn't made Eric Allen an offer but Baltimore had.

About that time, late April, I exercised a prerogative that all C.F.L. coaches use often – putting a guy on the recallable waiver list. This gives a reading on interest in him throughout the league but the coach is prepared to withdraw him and discuss a deal if anyone claims him. I put Dave Raimey on waivers. And we also had Thornton on a different times and nearly everybody on our team, so it's no disgrace.

I got in the office one morning. Luckily, Barrow was home with the 'flu. Otherwise he'd have been handling things. Margaret Wilson, the club secretary, told me that Hamilton had picked up Raimey. Now, I know how Sazio thinks over in Hamilton, and their money situation; they throw nickels around like manhole covers. Jerry Williams was brand new there at the time on the coaching staff.

I said, "Well, that's great. Raimey has a no-cut contract. If Hamilton picks him up, they have to pay him full salary for the year whether they want to use him or not."

I had an idea of what had happened. Jerry Williams would remember Raimey from away back, when Raimey was a star in Winnipeg and Williams was coach in Calgary. He'd think, "Hell, he's worth the $350 waiver price just to bring to camp and look at." But he wouldn't know about the high-priced no-cut contract.

I thought I saw something. I went to Lew Hayman and told him I thought I could get Eric Allen. Told him the circumstances and that I knew this was Barrow's responsibility but he was home sick and I didn't believe he could handle it anyway. "Let me do it," I said. He said to go ahead and try.

I called up Jake Gaudaur, the football commissioner and said, "Jake, Hamilton has picked up Dave Raimey. He's on a no-cut contract so they're committed to that contract."

He said, "Leo, I don't think Jerry Williams knew about that." But I reminded him of the rule that a coach could re-search a player's contract before deciding to pick him up and if Williams hadn't done so it should be no concern of ours. I said, "You're not going to rule that they don't have to take him, are you?"

He said he'd have to think about it.

"Let me call Jerry Williams," I said. So I called Jerry Williams and told him. He was shocked. "A no-cut contract? You're not going to stick me with that, are you?"

I said, "Jerry, you know better than to pick up a guy without researching his deal. But I'm not going to hold a gun to your head. I'll take a player off your negotiation list and call it even."

He was grateful. "Would you do that?"

"I'd be glad to," I said. He didn't know how glad.

"Who do you want?" he asked.

I said I'd call him back. Then I called Jake again. Went over the ground, that Hamilton would have to take Raimey if I insisted on it but said, "Look, I'll take a player off their negotiation list and call it quits."

"Let me call Jerry," he said. In about 15 minutes the phone rang and Jerry said, "I just talked to Jake. Which player do you want?"

I said, "I'll take Eric Allen."

He said, "Okay, he's yours. Make the arrangements." So I went to the commissioner's office and had the switch made, putting Eric on our list.

Later, when Sazio came back from Europe he was livid. I would have been, in his place. On past performance, anyway, we were already the team to beat. And now we'd not only got Eric Allen off his negotiation list but we'd kept Raimey. While Sazio might not have been able to sign Allen in a battle with Baltimore himself, he knew damn well that we might.

I got him on our negotiation list about 4 p.m. that day. At 4.30 Rountree and I were in the car headed for East Lansing, Michigan, to spend the evening with our new prospect. We took him out to dinner along with Jimmy Ray, who'd been a quarterback at Michigan State and now was an assistant coach. He was Eric's confidant and adviser.

Although we got along fine, Eric was kind of hot and cold. Baltimore had been to see him and naturally had made an impression, with more to come, because they never made a final offer at the first meeting, or anything like final. They were due back soon for another talk.

I knew I had to overcome another thing. Hank Bullough, who had been linebacker coach at Michigan State, was now with Baltimore. I knew how close Hank was to his old boss at Michigan State, Duffy Daugherty. If there was a choice I thought Duffy would try to steer Eric to Baltimore. I was thinking all this as we were finishing dinner that night. So I had a shot.

"Eric, it is your responsibility to at least visit Toronto and look around and meet some of our people. I won't even talk money with you, but I want to take you back to Toronto with me. Just show you around the city."

Jimmy Ray was suspicious. He said, "You're not going to talk contract when you get there? Not going to try to talk him into anything?"

I said, "I give you my word."

He said, "Eric, you hear that now." And Eric said he did.

So Rountree and I and Eric the next morning headed back to Toronto. We could have flown but I wanted to get the kid in the car with us. In the four or five hour drive we could talk, have a hamburger together, shoot the breeze together, do all these things that help people get to know one another. When we got to Toronto I took him to my house and met Shirley and the kids and then showed him around town. He met Stillwagon, Ed Harrington, and a few others. At the Argonaut Rowing Club he was applauded when he walked in. He liked it. He stayed an extra day. But then he wanted to get back and I did, too. The prelim was over. I wanted to get down to the nitty-gritty.

We got back in the car and drove to East Lansing again. We had driven there, driven back, and were on the road again, all in about three days. Eric drove some this time. At Michigan State he took me to his apartment and I met his girl friend. Then we met for dinner, with Jimmy Ray along, and we got more specific about money.

There was another man they wanted in on the discussions, Jim Ruttman, manager of a hotel in East Lansing. He was friendly with many of the football players and wanted to make sure Eric was making the right decision. For me, it seemed there were pitfalls everywhere. The hotel man was a close friend of Duffy Daugherty's. Duffy already had said Baltimore should have taken Eric in the first round of the pro draft instead of the fourth. He wanted Eric to go there and prove he'd been right. But we went over and met Ruttman at the hotel and talked to him. There I heard that a Baltimore coach was coming back to town, soon. I knew that if it was too soon we were going to lose this kid because he was too good a football player for Baltimore to back away from over a little money.

The next morning we were to go back to Ruttman's hotel, have breakfast with him, and then see a lawyer to talk about the legal end of the contract we were offering.

At 9 a.m. I'm sitting in the hotel. No Eric. It is 9.15 and still he doesn't show up. At 9.30 Jimmy Ray comes in. Jimmy says, "Where's Eric?" I said, "Hell, I don't know but I got a hunch Baltimore's in town and he's with them."

He said, "No, he's not with them."

He was so definite it gave me the strong impression that Jimmy had just left a Baltimore coach himself.

Then the door opens and in Eric comes. He'd slept in. I'd been sure we'd lost him.

After we had breakfast with Mr. Ruttman at the hotel, I said to Jimmy Ray, "Let's go over and see the lawyer." He hung back a little, strengthening the impression I had that he was leaning toward Baltimore for Eric. I said to Eric, "How about it?" And he said okay.

The law firm was Abood and Abood. The man we were to see was one of the senior partners, Frederic Abood. He called Eric and Jim by their first names. They said, "This is Mr. Cahill from Toronto."

"Toronto?" Abood said to Eric. "I thought you'd made up your mind to go to Baltimore." I thought, "Oh-oh."

Abood turned from them to me, "Let me go into the other room and talk to these two kids," he said. "I'll tell my secretary when I want you to come in."

I sat there for an hour. Every time the phone went I was sure they were on the phone to Baltimore. Any minute I expected the door to open and Baltimore to come walking in. But finally Abood came out. "All right, come on in," he said. We started negotiating. It was funny. Along in the conversation, when he found out I was head coach of the Argonauts and not an agent, the whole atmosphere changed. He hadn't realized I was the head coach, he said. He'd met Paul Brown once. We did some talking about Paul Brown. And the guy warmed up completely.

From that moment on we started getting down to cases. Tax structure. Injury clause. Other details. I didn't have any huge bankroll. Eric Allen was an afterthought as far as our budget was concerned. I wanted him badly but I couldn't spend a lot of money on the guy. I went as far as I could go and then Jimmy said, "I think he ought to have a car." I said, "What the hell, Jim, we've agreed on all this other stuff. What do you think, Mr. Abood?"

He said, "Jimmy, maybe you're putting too much pressure on the coach." He had swung over in my favor. Pretty soon we had reached an agreement. We signed the contracts, then and there.

There's one other point I want to make. The day before I'd told Jimmy Ray, "Look, win or lose on Eric, you've been a real good help to us." I was trying to influence him. I said, "When a guy really helps us with a player, whether we get him or we don't get him, we give the guy a couple of thousand dollars." I said I had this in the budget, $2,000 to give to him.

When it came right down to the final analysis, you don't find many people like Jimmy Ray. In the late stages of the negotiations he thought Eric should have $2,000 more. I said, "Jimmy, we're just out of money." He took me aside and said, "That couple of thousand dollars that you offered me, I wasn't going to take it anyhow, I was going to send it to Eric's mother. Take that $2,000 and put in on his contract." That was the $2,000 that swung the deal.

I mean . . . he was young too, with a young family and could use the money. Most guys can use $2,000 anytime. That was a really honorable move on his part.

I know for sure that Baltimore would have met or bettered our offer. No question about that. Coach Don McCafferty called me from Baltimore the following week and said, "You son-of-a-bitch."

I said, "What are you talking about?"

"Why, goddamnit, Allen!" he said. "You know we're not going to waste a high draft choice unless we need the guy. We had a guy right in town to see him and when he got there you had him signed."

I said, "Well, we need him too. Where were you going to use him? He'd be a specialist or something."

He said, "No. We were going to get into that triple option this year. This kid was going to be a big part of our offense." He ended up by saying, "Well, you did a good job, Leo. Congratulations." That's the kind of a guy McCafferty is. Incidentally, he later moved to be head coach at Detroit.

Back in May, getting ready for camp, I really thought we were set. I'd done a lot of thinking over the winter about not winning the Grey Cup. Defensively, we had young people in 1971, and they were going to be stronger – even Stillwagon, who'd been so good – because of the experience. Raimey had come along well in his first year on defense. Offensively, we were going to be stronger because Theismann and Barton had that year behind them. I figured that we needed more strength in the offensive line and potentially we had it now in Jackson and Mikolajczyk. We were going to have to suffer a little early in the season with the two young offensive linemen in there. But by the time the season ended, because of the personnel we had surrounding these young people, we should be strong enough to make the playoffs for sure and win it all.

One problem was that to play these two Americans in the offensive line, another American player would have to become vulnerable. We looked all over our personnel and finally came down to Mel Profit. We had two good Canadians playing at tight end behind Profit. Tony Moro had been a regular before and Bob Hamilton looked like he was going to come along. Between them we'd get the job done at tight end. That meant telling Profit that we were planning on playing a Canadian at his position, putting him out of a job. I felt that with a guy like Profit, who had made a large contribution to the team and was second to none with both fans and players, we owed it to him not to leave him dangling. He had threatened twice to quit football. One time he came back and played. The second time was after the Grey Cup game when he'd been quoted as saying he quit, had gone through enough of this aggravation. He hadn't gone through any more than the rest of us. He'd changed his decision over the winter, as pros often do, but it helped me make up my mind that I couldn't depend on him much longer.

I called Profit in and told him. I said, "I could have brought you to training camp and gambled against injuries and things like that. Hell, if things had worked out one way you might have played the position again and never have known your situation was in jeopardy. But I feel that because you have played well for us, I have to tell you."

He sat there and looked at me, in shocked disbelief. Finally he said, "I appreciate your telling me that."

I told him there were two ways to go. One would be for us to put him on waivers, so he could go to another football team.

He said, "I may change my mind but I don't feel right now that I want to play any place unless I play in Toronto. I'll get back to you and let you know."

The other thing I said was that he could just retire. "It then would be your own decision, not like being cut."

He decided to retire. He told the press that he couldn't fault me too much; at least I'd called him in and told him what we were going to do. There was a lot of talk about an article he'd written, or interview he'd given, criticizing the decision to install artificial turf in our stadium instead of spending it on widows and orphans, or something. Some reporters felt that when he'd done that, he'd made Bassett so sore that he told me, "Drop the s.o.b." There was nothing to that. It was strictly a judgement on my part that we had to play the two new imports on the offensive line and therefore needed a Canadian playing tight end. Meaning that Profit was out of a job. It's a perfect example of what coaches go through every year – maybe in not such publicity-making circumstances – because of the C.F.L. rule that allows 15 imports, no more.

It Should Have Been
Our Best Season

There must be a reason for the sun to come up in the morning and go down at night, and for a man to eat and get tired and sleep, so there must be a reason for the kind of football season we had in 1972. But it couldn't be seen in advance. The days were long gone when Argos had to depend on that us-against-the-world spirit that made them play over their heads. Now we were good enough to do what good football teams do: win on personnel and execution. Everybody in Canadian football could see that. We'd been in the Grey Cup the year before and many thought we were heading there again: this time to win it.

People said later I lost control of the team, my discipline was at fault, and a lot of other things. I feel myself that I did the best job of controlling the team that I'd ever done. During an incredible series of injuries, boob plays, rumors that I was about to be fired, singing of Goodbye Leo, and everything else we lost 11 games – eight of them close – and never collapsed. Even in the last game our guys played like wild men and never quit. But we were snake-bit all the way, starting right in training camp when Tim Anderson broke his leg badly, and Ed Harrington's right thigh, that had bothered him for years, was so bad he had to retire for that season at least.

The C.F.L. All-Star game was in Calgary in June. The rules are that the losing coach from the Grey Cup coaches the All-Stars, against the Grey Cup winner. I didn't like that system. It meant I had to leave my own camp for a few days at a most critical time and send four of my best players and one of my coaches, a week earlier; try to get ready for a season when everybody would be trying to knock us off while running the last part of the camp without Joe Theismann, Leon McQuay, Jim Corrigall, Paul Desjardins, and Blackie Johnston.

Leon was fighting something else right then. He blamed himself for what happened in the Grey Cup. He felt the fans were down on him because of it. I told him a dozen times that we wouldn't have been within 3,000 miles of Vancouver at Grey Cup time except for the way he'd played. But there was publicity at the time that when the going got tough he fumbled the ball, and other cliches that fans have. He lived with that and slept with it and sweated with it all winter long, and came back with a knee that still wasn't in good shape. When I went to Calgary a couple of days before the game I thought remarks made openly by many players at the All-Star camp might shake him out of it. They couldn't believe that there could be anyone like Leon McQuay, the way he could handle the ball and run sideways or forwards at full speed. Giardino from Ottawa and different players said to me they'd never seen anything to compare with him. But then he hurt his wrist very painfully and didn't play much. So that chance to restore his confidence was lost. And Jim Corrigall vaulted over top of somebody in the game and came down and somebody landed on his leg and broke it. He played most of the second half with the leg broken. I didn't let it out to the press even after the X-rays showed it. Just said that we were immobilizing a bad sprain in a cast so he would have to miss the exhibition games. But the rest of the players knew, and also knew how much we counted on Corrigall. The loss of Profit bothered some of them as well, more than I'd foreseen. We beat Hamilton 25-24 in our first exhibition game, but in the second were slaughtered by Ottawa and Ward Smith, who'd been making some sensational runbacks, broke his ankle. In our third exhibition game, in Winnipeg, John Trainor was in the warmup. He had done well at camp and we counted on him for the offensive line. We were about to go off the field for our pre-game meeting when he made a quick turn and went down. Blackie came to me in midfield and said, "Guess what?"

"What now?"

"Trainor's knee went."

McQuay was out, Smith, Corrigall, Harrington, Anderson, and now Trainor – as it turned out, for eight games.

When we came up to our first league game, at home against Montreal, we had a decision to make on McQuay's injury. If we put him on the 30-day injury list, he'd be gone for four games. We knew that if he was ready after the second game, his being in the ball game could mean 8 or 10 points to us. Maybe if we lost the first two games he'd come back for the second two and give us a lift. That was just guessing. All the other coaches felt that he should go on the 30-day list. Maybe they were right. They had me almost completely talked into that being the way to go, so we could use another American, maybe Bruce Bergey, who could play tight end, linebacker, or defensive end. Lew Hayman always came to our final personnel meetings. I turned to Lew and said, "What do you think?"

He said, "I'm a McQuay man. I always feel that he's a game-breaker. You may need him before the 30 days are up."

I said, "That settles it. I've been teetering. Let's go that way. So we counted McQuay on our roster although he wasn't going to play, and counted Corrigall knowing that he wasn't going to play. We went into the season really one Canadian short and one American short.

There was worse to come. In the sixth minute of that game against Montreal, Theismann went around right end from the seven for a touchdown. About five minutes into the second quarter, he went around right end again, was thrown for a one-yard loss and had to be helped off. On the bench, the doctor worked over his leg. Just the fact that he'd been taken off in pain lifted Montreal. They started to march with the ball. Then the doctor came up to me and said, "I think Joe's leg is broken."

The whole bench, to the last man, looked like they just lost

30 pounds in weight and six inches in height when they heard that word, broken. There was a quietness and a dullness.

I felt it. I grabbed Barton and said, "Okay, Greg, the torch has been passed. Now you gotta go in there and do a job. You know we can throw long against Montreal." He said, "Yeah, Coach, but let me start with the running game and get loosened up. I'll be all right, don't worry about it."

I said, "Okay, fine."

Meanwhile Montreal tied the game. In the first sequence Barton called nothing but the run, for Raimey and Eric Allen. But Greg had been pretty good the year before at exploiting the run, checking out people, then going to the deep pass. The second time he went in, he called a pass or two but nothing deep. When he came off the field a little later I was getting to the fever point. I grabbed him and said, "Goddamnit, you gotta throw the football deep. We gotta get back in this game. These players have gotta know that you are taking charge."

He said, "I couldn't, Coach. I heard Etcheverry yell to watch the pass." A coach will yell that a thousand times a game. I turned to Gibson and Rountree. They both looked at me the same way, as much as to say, "Oh my God! First game of the season, he's all we have and the guy doesn't want to do it."

He missed on sideline passes and looked bad. Some of the guys said that he was addled in the huddle. No take-charge at all. He was choking. But, as a great golfer one time said, "The guy who hasn't choked hasn't been in a position where he might choke." Everybody chokes. I felt it was just a matter of helping him get over that bad spot and playing himself into assuming the full responsibility. After all, this was the first time in many years that he'd had to shoulder all the responsibility alone.

But he looked very bad in that game. We lost it 19-8. Our total yards gained was 91 by rushing and 43 by passing. Barton completed five passes out of 19 for a total of 10 yards, with two interceptions. The morale of the team went that way, too.

However, the only little victory I had all that season came

after that game, although it worked out badly in the end, too. Bruce Bergey was a player we wanted to keep. To do so would mean dropping somebody else, maybe George Wells. Wells had been a starter in 1971 and we were reluctant to let him go. So we cut Bergey but still hoped to keep him around. I thought I might pay him his contract and send him to my friend Sam Handler, who ran Bramalea Satellites in the Ontario Rugby Football Union; sort of semi-pro ball. Then Bergey would be near if we needed him. But he suddenly decided to try Montreal – at about the exact time that I changed my mind and decided to keep Bergey and drop Wells.

The next morning our punter, Zenon Andrusyshyn, a close friend of Bergey's, told me where he had gone, and why. I was in my office at the stadium. I tried to get in touch with Bergey in Montreal before he got to the Alouettes. I called every hotel I could think of. I didn't call the Y.M.C.A. That's where he was. Finally I thought maybe he'd gone straight to the Alouettes office. If so I wanted catch him before they had an opportunity to sign him.

I called the Alouette office. I had to change voices. "Is Bruce Bergey there?" I asked. The secretary said, "Who is calling?" I said, "Mr. Bergey, his father."

The next voice I heard was that of my old friend and accomplice, J.I. Albrecht, who I thought for sure would recognize my voice. I went into one of my best other voices. I said, "Mr. Albrecht, this is Mr. Bergey and we're very concerned about Bruce. He told us that he was going to be playing in Toronto, but we understand that he's now in Montreal, and mother is quite upset. Could I speak to him?"

There was a long lull on the other side of the line. Then J.I. said, "Well, he's in a meeting."

I said, "If you'd just get him out and let me talk to him a couple of moments, I'd appreciate it." There was another long lull before he said, "Just a moment."

Knowing J.I., I could envision him going in to one of the extension phones to listen. When Bruce got on the line and said hello, I carried right through with the father gag in case J.I. was on the other line. Bruce knew it wasn't his father, of course, but I went through the routine of telling him that his mother was disappointed and had been talking to Coach Cahill, who said he was going to activate Bruce for the next game and wouldn't he rather play in Toronto?

Bruce said, "Yeah, I'd rather play in Toronto if I knew I was going to be activated." So I, still playing the father, said, "Well, rest assured that you will be activated for the next game. You're going to be part of the Argonaut team. Coach Cahill said that." That was as far as I could go, playing the father, but I hoped it would be enough.

That night I was having dinner with a prospect in Julie's restaurant. Bergey phoned Andusyshyn and said, "Listen, somebody called me and said it was my father. It wasn't but whoever it was told me I was going to be activated for the next Argo game. Do you think it could have been Coach Cahill?"

Andrusyshyn called my home. He and Shirley tracked me to Julie's and gave me Bergey's number in Montreal. I got him and told him to get his ass out of there and back to Toronto.

He said, "Are you sure? I have an opportunity to play here. I've already taken expense money. Should I give it back?"

I said, "Hell, no. Just get your stuff and get out of there. We'll send them back the money."

But he was honorable enough to go back and return them the expense money, before he left the following morning.

We started him the next game at Regina. That was our second with Barton in command. I still thought Greg could come on strong. Either he had the ability or I was wrong, Detroit Lions were wrong, and Philadelphia Eagles were wrong. But, well, if he had it at all he still couldn't produce it. We lost 15-6, then went home to play Ottawa. They won 14-8. We finished up with the ball on their nine-yard line after Barton threw two incompleted passes, either of which would have won it for us.

Montreal had dropped Jim Chasey at quarterback. We

picked him up. Then we went to play in Winnipeg August 23. Again we started Barton. He got one drive going that ended with an interception in the end zone. He got another going that ended with an interception. I tried Chasey. He passed for one touchdown to Bruce Bergey. Scrambled for another himself. We were alternating Barton and Chasey. On the third or fourth time of the alternating, when Barton should have been in, I looked up. There he was on the sidelines. I said, "Wasn't it your turn to go in?"

"Yeah," he said, "but Chasey was doing pretty good."

It just didn't seem like he wanted to play. It was so frustrating. I turned away from him. Right behind me was Norm Holland, my tailor, who had made the trip. I had to talk or I'd explode, but I couldn't say what I wanted to. I said, "Norm, when will my suit be ready?" He looked at me like I was crazy.

A little later in that game Bruce Bergey complained of feeling sick. He was turning blue, for God's sake. He damn near died. Couldn't get his breath. After the game he wound up in hospital and they found he had a lung injury and had to go on the injury list, so my phony voice routine hadn't done us much good in the long run.

Before that game ended, there was more frustration. We were leading and twice Zenon Andrusyshyn had chances for field goals, one from the 27 and the other from the 24. A few days earlier he'd kicked one from the 45, and several other longer ones, so we'd felt safe in cutting Ivan MacMillan and leaving Andrusyshyn to do the field goals as well as the punting. But he missed both times from perfect distances, and Winnipeg beat us 21-19.

After that game, our fourth loss in a row, John Barrow started looking for a coach to replace me. Barrow denied this but Bassett acknowledged later that it was true. Barrow was telling some reporters privately I was as good as gone. But Bassett defended me publicly, as he later did all season, pointing to all the injuries and generally backing me up. Barrow's early favorite as my replacement apparently was Bob Ward, an assistant who had quit Montreal and gone home. But Barrow told reporters before the Winnipeg game, supposedly in private, when we were only 0-3, that if he had to replace me now, he'd get Bernie Faloney for backfield coach, Bob Ward for line coach and he'd be the head coach himself. After three games – that griped my ass. He also told one reporter, Eaton Howitt of the *Sun,* a beer-drinking buddy of his, that I'd had a set-to with Barton and McQuay and that Stillwagon had asked me to be traded because of the concessions I was making to McQuay. This last was not true at the time, although Stillwagon complained to me about McQuay later. I had other troubles. I'd chewed out Jim Henderson at a workout. He was a Canadian with the ability to be valuable to us. I thought he needed to get mad at somebody and start catching passes as if he was mad. Instead, he quit the team.

I should mention, I guess, that I never had a direct confrontation with Barrow through all this. Only once did we come close. That was in Bassett's office when he asked me how the offensive line was grading out. I told him that Blackie graded the offensive line and that we'd figured on having break-in problems with the two Tampa rookies in there; but there was nothing we hadn't anticipated. He pulled out a ream of papers and said he'd been grading them and these were the grades they got. Hell, he couldn't make two zeroes the same size on a blackboard, how could he grade our line when in many cases he didn't know what their assignments had been? Maybe he was just trying to impress Bassett that he was head coach material in a pinch.

One thing Barrow did do well, though, was cultivate the young directors very assiduously. Not so much Johnny F., but young Lumbers and Burns and John Craig Eaton of the department store, newly named to the board. They didn't know much about football. He told me he was discouraging them from being in the way by coming to the dressing room or coming on trips, as directors sometimes like to do. I had the feeling he would rather have them as a captive audience than let them get to know me and understand my problems better.

Anyhow, that Winnipeg game was all for Barton. There were still years to go on that rich contract of his but it wouldn't be as a player. With me, anyway. Had things been different and we had more time I might have stuck with him but I was also getting a lot of heat from Bassett, who was definitely not a Barton man. Some felt later that the Barton situation was the final straw that broke my back – to spend a lot of money on a guy who just didn't deliver. But there was no time to stand around. I had a chance to get Wally Gabler again. Hamilton had traded him to Edmonton. He refused to report there but phoned to tell me he was available. I had to give Roger Scales to Edmonton to get him and hated to do it. Roger had scored our only Grey Cup touchdown and is a very coachable guy. Edmonton hadn't been going to get Gabler anyway and might have been a little easier on us. I guess they reflected on the Mike Eben situation of the year before, when I hadn't given them any breaks. So they stuck it to me good, demanding Scales.

Gabler knew our style and knew me. He'd beaten us when he was with Winnipeg and later with Hamilton. I thought after all the pressure of those years, he might come up big on another chance to prove himself in Toronto. Certainly he was the best quarterback available to help us out until Theismann got back.

It looked that way, too, in Ottawa at our next game. Gabler had been with us only two days. Chasey started and was moving the ball pretty good when he got hit on the head. He came off the field. He couldn't remember his plays. Gabler went in cold deck and played the rest of the game. That was the game he hit Leon McQuay right in the hands in the end zone and Leon dropped the ball. He hit Symons right in the hands wide open behind the Ottawa defensive backs and Symons dropped the ball and the sure touchdown. Andrusyshyn missed one field goal, then made one, but missed the extra point after our one touchdown, if you can believe this, and we lost the game 14-13. It was piling up. We'd missed two field goals the week before when we lost to Winnipeg, which came in the wake of leaving the ball on the nine-yard line against Ottawa. Now we go to Ottawa and drop two touchdown passes and miss an extra point, to get beaten by one point. If this is being out-coached, I'll kiss your foot. Even if we were then 0-5.

This brings us to Leon McQuay. He had played in all but the first game but his knee was bothering him and the fans were on him. So were some of the players. So was I. He'd missed a practice or two but it was with my permission. After all, he was hurt. But mainly his troubles were psychological.

He'd got lots of cheers the year before but now when he needed the confidence, really needed the fans to cheer, they booed him. He'd look up in the stands and think, These are the same people who were cheering for me last year when I was making all those yards and being called one of the greatest running backs who ever came to Canada. Now I'm limping on a bad knee and they're thinking I'm putting it on. That I'm not trying. That I'm through. All these thoughts were going through his mind.

When McQuay came to Toronto one player who befriended him and showed him around and kind of introduced him to Canadian football, at my direction, was Dave Raimey. Dave was the logical guy to do it. He had been a running back, exposed to great publicity himself and he had been a temperamental player in his formative stages. Being friends, at different times during the season they would kid back and forth. But they were also short-fuse guys. Sometimes the kidding would get out of hand and there'd be an argument. But that was Raimey's style. He was a constant baiter of everybody.

Now we're 0-5 and getting ready to play in Montreal on Labour Day. We had been put out of our own park by the Canadian National Exhibition and were working out at York University. We were edgy with all our problems. Earlier in the week I'd got on Leon about not running the right play on a handoff. He'd misunderstood something I'd told him and when he did it wrong again I told him, "Goddamnit, Leon. Do it this way."

He turned and barked at me, "You told me to do it the other way. Why don't you stay off me?" – which was a natural reaction for someone as undisciplined as he could be. But I shouted back at him to keep his mouth shut and be a football player. He apparently said something in the huddle about if I'd leave him alone he'd make a lot of yards but for any other coach he'd make more yards because I was always on his back. I didn't hear that until later. But it still had been a confrontation and since I'd let him get away with it I felt I had to explain to the rest of the team. I told them that all my life my style with football players had been discipline. That afternoon they'd seen me not enforce discipline. But the game coming up was more important than one individual so I was going to let it slide. This was the sort of thing they construed as me giving him too many breaks.

That happened during the week. Then there was an argument on the Saturday morning. Leon's girl friend was at the practice. She was from Miami. Raimey and Leon got kidding each other and then it got into a shouting match. I didn't see or hear it. I was late coming off the field, watching the kickers and specialists. Everyone else had gone into the dressing room. On the way, I went up to Leon's girl friend to chat with her about Leon.

She broke in, "Haven't you seen what's going on? There was the awfulest talking and the awfulest fight I ever saw between Leon and Raimey."

I got into the dressing room. Everything was over but Rountree told me that when he came in they were screaming.

Chip Barrett had got into the thing with Leon and at one point called to Raimey, "Can't you do anything with Leon?"

Leon said, "What the hell is this anyhow? Is this a football team or is this some kind of a racial situation where the blacks do for the blacks and the whites do for the whites?" Then Leon challenged Raimey to fight, same to Barrett, same to about four other people. There wasn't a taker. He was furious, standing on the bench with just his jock strap on when Rountree came in.

Rountree didn't know the background and he said, "Goddamnit, Leon. Stop it. Be still." Right away Leon thought Rountree was taking sides with the other people. But all Rountree had heard was Leon's tirade. It was a very tense situation before it quieted down.

When I heard the details, knowing what Leon had been going through before, I said to the coaches, "I wouldn't be surprised if Leon doesn't show up in Montreal." I knew he'd be deeply hurt. Raimey had always been close, a friend. To Leon it would be as if his whole world was collapsing around him.

He didn't show up for the plane trip. I really believed that the guy might have quit. When we got to Montreal I called Tony Razzano, his agent, in Dayton and said, "Tony, damnit, get hold of Leon and tell him to get to Montreal or I'm going to suspend him and put him out of football forever. He can't pull this kind of thing. Regardless of what his feelings are, he's got to be man enough to face the situation and mature with it."

Tony said, "I'll try."

Meanwhile, I had Gordie Ackerman call Pete Wysocki in Detroit and get him to Montreal. This was kind of a standard joke that season. This was about the third or fourth time. When something would go wrong we'd always bring Pete in. Our deal with him was that he'd stay in shape and be available. He'd be all hyped up and ready to play and at the last minute he wouldn't get a chance. But we slept that night and when we walked out of the breakfast room the next morning for the team meeting, who's waiting for me with the whole team but Leon.

I got up at the blackboard really upset. "Life is too short to spend all night worrying about one player, Leon," I said. "It is an automatic fine right now, $500, for what you did. Now what I want to know is, are you ready to play football or are you not?"

I found out later that the players construed even this as a concession on my part, because I gave him a choice instead of suspending him.

205

He said, in a very grumpy way, "Yeah, what do you think I'm here for?"

After the meeting I kept him there and he and I had another of the scores and scores of talks that we'd had over the two years. At the end he said, "I'm going to go out there and I'm going to show you today. We're going to win this game because I'm going to show you. I'm going to be the best I've ever been."

I said, "Well, that's fine, but after today let's not go through the same routine again." And from then on he never did get out of line. Right to the end of the season.

He went out there in Montreal and played just like he'd promised. He got our first touchdown on an 18-yard pass from Gabler in the first quarter. In the second quarter he took a handoff and went 50 yards, setting up a touchdown pass to Mike Eben. In another series he had runs of six, 15 and eight to set up a field goal by MacMillan, whom we'd activated again. Leon later took a 43-yard pass from Chasey for another touchdown. On the day he had 129 yards rushing and 64 on passes. Gabler and Chasey were working well. Eric Allen scored two touchdowns, one a 52-yarder after a pass. I thought we were back on the rails again but I was especially happy about McQuay's super day. All season long he had worried about his knee, the fans, his future, the other guys not liking him, and was it worth it, beating his head off? Then that day he got so mad, disgusted, and fed up that he was going to show us all. When he got out there and did the things that he was capable of doing, he must have gone home and thought, "My knee isn't so bad after all." He was okay from there in.

After the game we went into the locker room. Charlie Bray presented me with the game ball and said, "You stuck with us through all this stuff. Now we're going to go from here and win all the rest." Bassett was in the dressing room. There was the feeling that we finally had played ourselves out of this thing. We could see in the future Theismann coming back. Gabler had played a great game for us. McQuay had passed the crisis, maybe one of the big turning points in his life. It looked like everything was coming our way.

It was, too – until the following week, when we were leading Hamilton 11-0 and a punt went to Elmars Sprogis on our 11-yard line. He fumbled. On the sidelines Rountree and I groaned, oh my God, we were going to give Hamilton one of those cheap touchdowns. He picked the ball back up. We breathed a sigh of relief. But then he circled back all the way from the 11 into the end zone and fumbled again. Tony Gabriel fell on it for a touchdown. In the fourth quarter we were leading 18-14 but Hamilton was pressing us and we needed something to get out of our own end. So we tried a fake quick kick and screen pass. I told Gabler to make sure he played it safe. He faked the quick kick and threw the screen pass to Leon. It was a little high. Leon jumped but only deflected the ball. It came down in Bruce Smith's hands, the Hamilton defensive lineman. He ran it to our six-yard line and in the next play they scored to come from behind and beat us 22-18.

That was the most discouraging loss of my career. It ruined the momentum we'd taken out of the Montreal game. The next week B.C. Lions beat us 23-9 in the game I outlined in Chapter One, the Goodby Leo chorale. The wolves were really howling for my scalp. One of the worst was Danny Nykoluk, who by then had a radio show where people phoned in to comment after a game. The callers Nykoluk loved were the ones who criticized the offensive line, especially his old position, offensive tackle. When he wasn't running down Ron Mikolajczyk, he was praising the defensive ends who played against him. Nykoluk was particularly scathing about this a few days later when Hamilton massacred us 41-14.

But there was more. On September 30 Edmonton came in. Maybe you're getting as tired of this catalogue of disasters as I am but if losing football games by incredible means can be called an art form this one would lead the field.

We had Joe Theismann in uniform for the first time in eight weeks but Gabler started the game. Tom Wilkinson started for Edmonton and early on he passed to Bobby Taylor for a 28-

yard gain just to remind the fans of the old Argos of a few years before. We were losing 7-4 in the second quarter when I sent Theismann in. Suddenly everyone could see what we might have been if he'd been healthy all along. A pass to Bill Symons went for 12, another to Eric Allen for 15. Theismann ran for six, passed to Symons for another 15, passed to Allen for the touchdown. Zip, zip, zip – and we're ahead. Right back, as soon as we got the ball again after the kickoff, Theismann passed to Symons for 18, threw one incomplete for Allen, completed one to Moro for 18, lost 11 on a tackle by Greg Pipes, threw to McQuay for a gain of 31, missed Eben, threw to Allen for 19 and then another into the end zone for Eben. Touchdown again. Already he'd made nine passes good of 11 thrown, for 143 yards and two touchdowns.

His leg wasn't completely right and he hurt it again in the third quarter, running right end. All the same, we had Edmonton 26-14 when the fourth quarter began. We got a field goal but Wilkinson threw two touchdown passes, the second a 30-yarder to Bobby Taylor, to cut our lead to 29-28. With 99 seconds to go Dave Cutler kicked a field goal from the 40 and they won it 31-29. We had 29 first downs to their 15; picked up 481 yards to their 291. But lost. That night I also lost my poise, completely. I blew up at Lew Hayman, who'd always been friendly to me, and said many things I regretted later, berating him for sanctioning the pressure that was on me. I told him I couldn't justify his allowing Barrow to be out recruiting coaches. I cussed everyone in the organization. That was where I lost Lew. I heard that he phoned Bassett a few days later and said he no longer was interested even in coming out to our practices, they were so listless. When I lost Lew, I lost my most valuable ally.

A little later Barrow made a move that would have been funny if it hadn't been so sad. The year before, I'd been named Coach of the Year. This award was by an annual vote of the coaches. Norm Kimball in Edmonton sent the 1972 ballot to Barrow with a note saying to have me fill it out. Barrow filled it out himself and sent it back. Kimball got on the phone and said Barrow had misunderstood, that this was a poll of coaches. Barrow should talk it over with me, Kimball said. If I disagreed with the votes he'd cast in my place, we should get back to Kimball. Barrow never mentioned it to me at all, one way or the other. Nothing.

When I picked up the paper one morning and read that Jack Gotta at Ottawa was 1972 Coach of the Year, my successor, I phoned Kimball.

I said, "I appreciate that Jack Gotta did a good job this year but I would like to have had a vote."

He said, "What do you mean you would like to have had a vote? You had a vote." And he told me the story. Making this incident public, or protesting about it, might have cast a smirch on Gotta's award. So I kept quiet and simply stored it away as another Barrow incident.

Besides, the team was my main concern. The amazing thing was, we still had a chance to make the playoffs. Early in October Montreal had won only four games and if they flopped – which they did – and we won three, including our next game against them, we could tie them and go into the playoffs on the basis of having beaten them twice in our three meetings. We beat them 21-3 on October 8, the game we had to win to make it work. We went to Calgary the next week and won 33-27. Theismann was getting stronger. Dave Cranmer was in better shape after his abdominal surgery. Corrigall was right again. We had a chance.

But in our next game we were leading Ottawa 16-14 with 47 seconds left when there was a fantastic catch by Hugh Oldham. After he made it he was falling, off balance, when two of our defenders hit him at the same time from opposite sides and kept him on his feet to squirt out from between them and score the touchdown that beat us 21-16.

In that game Dave Raimey broke his hand. Now we were down to one game, in Hamilton. We had to win if we were going to make the playoffs. Hamilton had won 10 and lost three, the exact opposite of our three and 10. I was under no illusions. Hamilton was good. Their rookie quarterback, Chuck Ealey, was playing like a veteran. I'd tried to rattle him in one game but he took it all. The game loomed right then as the most important of my career.

I could write a whole book on that Hamilton game alone. Herb Solway, who had been talking to Bassett, warned me that if we lost, I'd be fired the next day.

Our game preparations were a classic dilemma of personnel selection. The defensive cornerback position, which Dave Raimey played, is the most demanding in football next to the quarterback. The cornerback has the constant job of covering the other team's best receivers, one on one. Jimmy Dye had played the position before. We were lucky there. But could he step in and adjust to it again in only a few days? Also he'd been playing very well for us at safety. We needed his strength there, too, or someone just as good. For another safety, where could we go? Tim Anderson, the first-round draft choice of San Francisco who'd played very well for us in 1971 had broken his leg badly in the 1972 training camp. He had been on the injury list all season; the 30-day first and then four times on the 15-day list. His last time would end before the Hamilton game but, after being out all season, could he play?

I delayed making the decision right down to the final day before the game, so we could look at Tim all week in practice. Meanwhile we decided that if he couldn't play we would move Marvin Luster from middle linebacker to rover, and move Peter Paquette over to safety. Then we would have to worry about who was going to play middle linebacker. We'd paid Pete Wysocki in Detroit to lay out for the season and to keep active in case we needed him. My main concern was his physical condition. Could he come in and play well in this key situation? He hadn't played all season long. Would he have the timing, the ability to fit in? In the end we decided we'd go with Tim Anderson at safety, Dye at cornerback and leave the rest of the lineup as it was.

The overpowering stress as far as I was concerned was my conversation with Herb Solway. It kept coming back to me, echoing and re-echoing in my head: if you lose this game, Monday you'll be called in and be fired. The more I thought about Timmy Anderson coming off the bad fracture, the more I thought about Jimmy Dye playing cornerback for the first time in several games, the more I thought about the overall picture, the more apprehensive I became. It was difficult to sleep. Still, I had to portray to the players a strength and conviction that we could win.

A couple of things I've often reflected on since happened in the few days before that Hamilton game. One was a dinner for Schenley Award selectors, when the Eastern candidates were announced. One of those at the head table as an Argonaut director was Len Lumbers, Sr. I was asked to speak. I said a few words about the season we'd had and that I hoped I'd be around to show what this team we'd put together could do some year when it was healthy. I heard later that behind me, as I said those words, Lumbers was sitting there grinning at the audience and shaking his head.

The other time was two or three days before the Hamilton game. Johnny F. Bassett came down to the stadium one night, something he'd never done before. He had a tux on. He came in my office and stood around and looked at me. I had the feeling he wanted to tell me something. I didn't know what. I found out later that he was going to Europe and wouldn't be home for whatever was about to happen to me. In his own way I think he wanted to show that sentimentally he still had a feeling for me even though he knew better than anybody – he was part of it – how the odds were stacked against me. He'd been the one who said after our fourth or fifth game that if it was a matter of a democratic vote, I was out. But this night he didn't have anything to say. We exchanged a couple of pleasantries. Then he had to go back to the Royal York for some function. There was no reason for him to come down there, but he did.

211

I went to the Seaway Hotel on the morning of the game. The players knew this was do-or-die for me. The tension about our pre-game meal and approach to the game was more threatening, more ominous even than it had been for the Grey Cup the year before.

We ate quietly and didn't have much to say. We knew what we had to do. We got on the bus and headed for Hamilton. I can remember getting off the bus in front of the locker rooms to lead the team in through the gate. I was met there by a lady wearing the Argonaut double-blue. I was happy to see somebody wearing those colors. Then she spoke. "One thing for sure," she said, "we're not going to have to put up with you again next year."

We went into the dressing room and started preparing. There was none of the usual buzz. The only sound was from the five or six guys who always went into the bathroom and vomited before a game. Time seemed to last forever, as if we'd never get the call to hit the field for the pre-game practice. Then we did.

As we walked out on the field to take the far end zone to start our calesthenics, we had to pass the Hamilton team. Two players I had coached, Blum and Gary Inskeep made derogatory remarks to me on the way past. I kept right on going. As I reached the 50-yard line heading down into the end zone, all of a sudden the fans from Hamilton took up the cry, Goodbye Cahill.

When I watched the players catch the ball and run through ball handling, I had the feeling that we were going to make that supreme effort. That we were mentally prepared if not physically prepared. When the game began we scored first, on a Theismann pass to Eric Allen. Then they got a couple and Allen scored again. We manhandled Hamilton physically. There was real hitting. Where we were standing on the sidelines, the bitterness transcended any earlier Hamilton-Toronto game. I think that the Hamilton people, the Hamilton bench, the trainer, and everyone else sensed that if they beat us today they were going to be done with me. When we left the field at half time trailing 25-13, their trainer, Jim Simpson, came up and challenged me openly, saying, "You hotdog son-of-a-bitch," and that he'd do this and that to me. I turned around in amazement. The guy is old. I could have hit him with a backhand and knocked him flat. It was almost to the funny stage that this guy, their trainer, hated me so much.

In the second half, we couldn't do it. Theismann, who had come off the broken ankle five weeks before, was still not right. That Hamilton kid from Michigan State, Al Brenner, made five interceptions. And Timmy Anderson who had worked so hard all week in preparation couldn't make himself go on the ankle. The week of running actually seemed to have weakened it. He just couldn't make himself run.

All of a sudden there were only a couple of minutes left in the game. The score was 26-16. There was no way that we could win. I just got that sick feeling that no matter what I'd done it was all over.

After the game I went with the other coaches to the Seaway. We broke out a case of beer and some sausages and sat by ourselves and talked. The others wanted to get home to their wives. They were saying to me, "Come on out to the house. Be with us." I just didn't want to let them go. We'd been through this whole thing together. I just wanted to sit there and see if there wasn't some way, if we drank long enough, that the picture could change. But I knew it couldn't.

So I called Shirley and we went out to Rountree's house for the rest of the wake. On Sunday I went to mass but not to St. Clement's, my own parish, where I'd be amid people who knew me and would be saying, "Well, you lost the game. What next?" I went to another parish a couple of miles away.

I've always had a good healthy respect for the church and I think every coach is a little bit superstitious. For instance, I felt one of the reasons why things went bad in my last year was that my dad died. He was a very devout man, said the rosary every day, and always had my welfare so much at heart. I used to wonder, when everything went bad, how many points those prayers of his had counted for.

I don't recall if I ever discussed that or not with my own best friend in the priesthood, Father Dan McLarnon. He is a Jesuit and he'd been around our dressing room a lot and sometimes brought a rabbi or a Protestant minister – any man of the cloth was okay with me. For some reason I never felt that I could stand on my own two feet as far as my association with the Almighty was concerned, that I always needed help from any place that I could get it.

So, as I said, I went to church. At home later I tried to put my best foot forward with the kids but they kept asking me, "Are you going to get fired? Is this the end? You don't think they'll really fire you?" What could I say? But I put them off.

"I Had to Tell Them It Was All Over"

On Monday I came in to the main Argonaut offices in the Richmond-Adelaide Centre. This was the office I wasn't in much during the season. I wanted to get it over. I couldn't take another minute of this apprehension. Soon the call came that I was expecting, from Bassett's male secretary. But what he said was, "Could you be in Mr. Bassett's office at ten o'clock on Thursday morning?"

My God, Thursday morning! I have to go through three more days of this?

I had to talk to somebody so I went up to see Herb Solway. My office was on the 6th floor and he's on the 15th in the law firm of Goodman and Goodman. Bassett's office was on the 12th floor of the same building. He'd moved there after he closed the *Telegram* at the end of October, 1971.

When I hit the elevator in the Richmond-Adelaide Centre that day I thought back to 1965, with my family waiting in a motel to hear if I got the Rifles job. That was the first time I met Herb. Then I thought back to 1967 when I took this same elevator up to the 15th floor to tell Herb that I was going to the Argonauts. At that time he was a director of the Rifles. With Herb it was always more than business. He'd remained a close friend through the years. Anything strictly football I'd talk over with the coaches. But away from the Argonauts, the two opinions that I always solicited were Herb's and Shirley's. He could always add an extra dimension seasoned with logic and insight.

When I went to Shirley, if what I had to tell sounded good to her, I was sure it was right. If she said, "That doesn't sound like you," I'd know it was wrong.

When I told Herb that Monday that I had to be in Bassett's office on Thursday at 10 a.m. he said to let him check it out. He'd find out what was on Bassett's mind, why Thursday instead of now, and so on. If he didn't call me earlier we'd talk about it on Wednesday. Bassett liked Herb and respected him. Anything he told Herb was going to be pretty well the way it was.

When Herb called me on Wednesday and asked me to come up to his office, I didn't run to consult my zodiac guide. I knew that it was game over. If there had been any good news, any hope at all, Herb would have told me on the phone.

When the elevator stopped at the 15th floor, I suddenly felt embarrassed. Embarrassed for Herb because he was going to be giving me the bad news, embarrassed for myself because all of a sudden I realized that people would be feeling sorry for me. I was completely ready for anything but sympathy.

In Herb's office, he made an attempt to be deeply engrossed in his own affairs. He was pale around the gills, more subdued than I can ever remember seeing him. But he got right to the point and told me they were going to call me in and fire me. He had gone to Bassett the day before. When he heard what was to be done, he told Bassett that he was making a terrible mistake, and urged him to reconsider.

Bassett told him that even if he'd wanted to reconsider, it was too late. The directors had met. That had been one reason for the three-day delay, the directors' meeting. They had decided to fire me. Herb asked me to come back to him the next day before I went to see Bassett. "I'll let you know if anything has changed," he said. "But I don't think anything will change."

I went home and told Shirley. We decided not to tell the kids. We didn't want to bring it out until it was final.

I got up early the next morning after not sleeping much. In fact, I hadn't slept much for a week by then. Normally I could always sleep even when I had a lot on my mind. I'd never get up and pace and eat or drink, as some others do, and I've never taken a sleeping pill in my life. I could usually lie there in the darkness and think and finally fall asleep. This particular week I'd lie there and think and sleep wouldn't come.

Shirley was aware what day it was. The whole family was aware. I got up and put on a new checkered suit. I had adopted, after a lot of thought, the philosophy that I had nothing to be ashamed of. I'd done more for the Argonauts as a team and a business than anyone had for a long time, if ever. I'd made a contribution to the league, by bringing in exciting players. So I would face this guy and have my final say. I was going to talk to him freely, the way I felt. If he didn't like it, well, I'd been his audience a few times and I hadn't always liked that either.

I went to Herb's office. Herb said, "He'll be meeting you at 10 o'clock. Lew Hayman is going to be there."

I said, "Like hell Lew is going to be there. Bassett always told me that if he was going to fire me, he was going to fire me by himself. He isn't going to cop any pleas now and have Lew Hayman sitting in there to take the stress and strain off what I have to say."

"Well, that's what he's planning on doing," Herb said.

I grabbed the phone and called down to Margaret Wilson in the Argo office. I said, "Margaret, I want to talk to Mr. Bassett."

She said, "Leo, I'm afraid you can't. He's with the directors right now."

I said, "Margaret, do me a favor, will you? Get him on the phone."

She broke into the meeting and got him on the phone. I said, "Mr. Bassett, I understand that in our conversation at 10 o' clock, Lew Hayman is going to be sitting in."

He said, "Yeah, that's to make it official because he's the club president. Isn't that all right with you?"

I said, "No, it's not all right with me but if that's what you've made up your mind to do, I suppose I'll have to accept it." I thought of the many phone calls from him in the past where he'd just hang up the phone before I could speak after he'd said his piece. I hung up the phone before he could say a word.

Ten o'clock was closing in. I got on the elevator, went down to the 12th floor, said hello and smiled at a battalion of news people waiting to see what was going to happen. I was damned if I was going to lose my poise today. I almost had to chuckle when I noticed Mel Profit, who by then was sports director of a television station. I found out later that Mel was making book that when I got in there and put the thing in perspective, Bassett wouldn't fire me. This was kind of a compliment. He was a guy who knew the score and the way I operated, even though we were very different people.

I walked in. Bassett's secretaries were there. They looked like they'd been at a wake themselves.

I walked into the inner office, which is smaller and less imposing than the one he had at the *Telegram*. That one had a penthouse atmosphere. A lot of the furnishings and pictures were the same; his family, the Kennedys, and so on. Lew was sitting at the left of Bassett. I sat to Bassett's right. He started talking.

I had made up my mind I was going to be as tough on him as possible. I wanted to keep full control of myself even though I was under heavy emotional stress and knew it. I sat opposite him, crossed my legs, folded my arms and looked right at him. For 15 minutes he explained to me why the directors had come to this conclusion. It was based completely on the season we had this year. It had nothing to do with any reflection on me as an individual. He thought I was a fine person, a fine football coach. This was the most difficult decision he'd ever had to carry out, in his life, other than closing down the *Telegram*. He just kept talking. He would look at me, look away, come back to me again. I hadn't blinked, even. The more he talked the more repetitious he became. Then he started stuttering. I kept looking at him. Finally, he lowered his voice and turned to Lew and said, "Is there anything else, Lew?"

Lew said, "I guess that pretty well covers it, John."

He said, "Do *you* have anything to say, Lew?"

Lew said, "No."

There was a silence. I said, "Is this all you have to say, Mr. Bassett?" He said yes. "Does this cover the legal part of the meeting?" I asked. He said yes.

I said, "Well, then, I'd like to have my moment with you, because I've had plenty of time with Lew Hayman in the past."

He said, "Well, fine. Okay, Lew, we'll see you later." Lew got up and scurried out of the room.

I got on my feet and confidence began to flow. You have an inner strength when you feel you are right. It took 20 to 30 minutes, what I had to tell him. I had it all in my mind: what Argos were when I came, how many season tickets they had sold, how many games they were winning a season. How Argonauts were the laughing stock of football. And how we changed all that.

He sat at his desk in a subdued way. For the first time through all the years that we'd been together I was the talker. I knew that I was on my way out but I wanted to make him feel as I had felt. As I went over the record I even emulated his style, the things he used to go through for effect when he was talking to me or a player that I'd brought in. I strode back and forth with my thumbs on my belt. I opened my coat and let it fly behind me as I walked. I went over to the Kennedy pictures and stood there six inches away and looked at the pictures as I talked to him. The whole routine.

He just sat there and let me have my say. He could afford to.

I have to admit that never once did he change the attitude that this was the toughest decision he'd ever had to make and how badly he felt. I almost ended up feeling sorry for him. But tomorrow he'd still have his life as before.

There was one time in the conversation I became overwrought and emotional. That was when I said, "The thing that really bothers me about this whole thing is not what I've done. I know that I've done a job for you and for the city and for the league in general. The only thing I feel bad about is for my family, my wife and my kids, to have them think that I've failed." When I said that, I felt control going. I goddam bit my tongue. When I tasted the salt, the control came back and I went on from there. I had one more shot I wanted to fire.

Summarizing all the achievements, along with what he'd said this morning about me, I said, "If this is true and all the good you said about me is true and you still want to fire me, I have to conclude that you should get an Academy Award for the show you put on this morning, or it is a fix." He knew what I meant: a fix based on Barrow and his little troupe of directors who didn't know whether a football was round or square. "Barrow had nothing to do with it," he said. "We don't have him make decisions like this."

There wasn't much more. He had mentioned that my contract would be fulfilled. It ran for two more years. I said that the other coaches, who were going down with me, had families and apartments and bills. Their contracts would run out January 1, a few weeks away.

I said, "If you are going to do this, give them at least six months' pay so that they can get something else." He picked up the phone, got Lew, and said, "Lew, give the coaches an extra four months." So I at least got that for them.

After everything was said, I walked out and he followed me. We walked through the door and there was this whole group of news people waiting there. I told them that I disagreed with what Bassett had done but he'd fired me. Bassett and I talked back and forth. That's when he admitted publicly for all to hear that Barrow had been checking out Bob Ward as coach even while denying there were plans to replace me. I answered about as many questions as I could. In the papers the next day they said I'd kept my composure and handled things well. But when I was talking to everyone there in the hall, microphones, cameras and pencils, all of a sudden I excused myself and said I wanted to go the bathroom. When I rounded the corner toward the bathroom, suddenly I had a completely empty feeling. It was all over. I felt very badly. I went down the backstairs and drove around for a while. I stopped at a pay phone to call Shirley and tell her that it was official. It would be in the papers and on the radio so she should tell the kids. I said I was going to be by myself for a while and think about the thing and then go to the stadium and meet the coaches and tell them what the story was, because they were waiting there for me.

One thing that really worried me right then was that my oldest son, Steve, was away in North Bay at school. He was going to hear this all of a sudden. I called him and told him about it and told him not to worry, I had opportunities to go elsewhere, we'd be fine. And if anybody said anything to him about it, he was to say, "To hell with you. We're going to be much better off." I got to him before the whole thing hit him.

I spent about half an hour just riding around thinking. When I walked into the stadium the coaches were all waiting, I think they hadn't given up believing that maybe I was going to wave a wand and stop the whole thing. I had to tell them it was all over.

Eppie was there, too, in the catacombs he'd guarded like a tiger after so many games, all the ones I'd been there for. He said things would never be the same and this was probably the end of him, too. I said, "Listen, Eppie, if I stabbed you right now you'd bleed double blue. I'm going to be gone but your real connection with the Argonauts is the players themselves. They're still here. So will you be. And don't feel bad." But he did.

Then reporters started coming in and we sat around talking about the past. George Gross, sports editor of the *Sun*. Jim Proudfoot who has the same job at the *Star*. Some of the others I'd seen earlier outside Bassett's office; faces behind microphones or cameras. Bill Stephenson from CFRB. John Badham from CFTR, who I saw every day for most of the year because of the radio show we did together. Fergie Olver from CFTO.

CKEY's big, quiet Jim Hunt. Don Chevrier and Tom McKee from C.B.C. Larry Wilson from CHUM. Jim Coleman, Esaw, Marsden, Walker, MacLeod – pardon the list. That day I felt that these guys I'd worked with so closely professionally for six years turned out also to be my friends, concerned for me.

After everybody left I stayed in the stadium for a couple of hours, talking and thinking. Rountree said, "When you walked in and told us, I thought of all the times when you walked into this room and said, 'Okay, let's go!' " To games and practices. Blackie philosophized that this was a crazy business and he didn't know why any of us were in it, except that we're in it for the good years when nothing is important but the games. Gordie said, "It just doesn't seem possible that we won't be in here any more, to do this and do that, putting the thing together." We agreed that maybe in a year it would seem we'd never been there at all.

Then I just went home. I got there about dinner time. My kids were all crying. But I think really what they were worried about, after our lives together revolving around football, was how I'd be taking it. They felt the world just couldn't do that to their father. They couldn't wait to see the look on my face. If it had been sad or crushed I don't know what the hell they might have done. But I knew that. I walked in and said, "Well, I was looking for a job when I got this last one. Now we'll go down and probably coach in the National Football League. Win the championship. Go to the Super Bowl." Then they were all happy. The main thing with them was what I was going to think, what my reaction would be. It had been tough for them. But just as people who'd never been friendly before came up to me and said this was a gross injustice, and we're for you, and what can we do to help you? . . . the kids who sang Goodbye Cahill to my kids turned around and practically went into mourning with them.

I think before that final day, because of all the publicity I got, the image of being a wise-guy and a know-it-all, many people secretly or openly were hoping that I'd get my comeuppance, get knocked down. But when it happened the news media and people on the street and letter-writers and a lot of the same people who'd been against me, suddenly said, "Jesus, this shouldn't have happened." It was like, this is a nice guy, too bad he died. People always save those things for when it is too late. The kids probably were better liked the day I got fired than at any time before since I was head coach. You know. Human nature. There's a common good in all people. The other kids could sense that all of a sudden Cahill's father wasn't a big shot any more and how this must hurt. Or maybe their parents told them to be nice.

Goodbye Argos

I want to finish up with a few personal musings. I've now had much of a year to think, while I decide what to do with the rest of my life. The first month after I was fired, I had to go back to my home town – in the way I'd sent so many players in the past – and tell the people, no, I'm not there any more, I was cut, I got the axe. I had a few football offers, both sides of the border. Right away my name was mentioned as a possible successor to Sam Etcheverry in Montreal. Columnists and commentators there extolled by record – the same record that couldn't save my job in Toronto – as being exactly the kind of exciting, building, crowd-attracting performance that was needed to make the Alouettes into a football power again. As soon as I heard about it I called a press conference and said no. How could I come off the season I'd had and then offer myself as part of the knife aimed at the back of another coach? Even if we weren't friends. A Hamilton sportswriter told me that Sazio phoned Sam Berger, the Montreal owner, and advised him not to hire me because I was bad for the league. Add it up: we'd beaten Hamilton badly, out-smarted them on Eric Allen, and insisted on paying Canadian players decent salaries. Any one of those things would put me on Sazio's no-no list. All three of them he couldn't take at all.

One job I would have accepted instantly: a little luncheon engagement to speak to owners and directors of C.F.L. teams and tell them a few things I'd learned, or had known all along.

224

"You have to understand that as sure as the sun rises in the morning you're going to have good years and bad years," I'd tell them. "But the way you should look at a coach when you're hiring him is: What kind of a person is he? Is he the guy we want to take our chances with, cast our lot with? And then if you decide yes, also be aware that it should never be a matter of one year but a good period of time. Five years. Six years. All to be balanced at the end in total, the good and the bad, when you're basing your decision on whether to embark on another period of time together." And on my own immediate behalf I'd say: "Also, don't let a coach put together a group of players who are capable of winning and then bring in another guy to capitalize on the hard work that has been done."

Around Grey Cup time in Hamilton, a group of people got together a dinner in Toronto for me and my coaches. They paid $20 a plate, 150 of them, to tell Blackie and Gord and Rountree and Cahill thanks for some good years. I told them the truth: that each morning when I woke I was torn between two things that I must decide, whether I wanted to live in Toronto, or wanted to be a football coach. And that each night when I went to bed I hadn't made the decision.

In February, a horse owner named Saul Wagman let it be known he was going to name a horse Goodbye Leo. An anonymous phone caller threatened to kill the horse and him if he did. His lawyer, Wagman said, had scolded him also for picking that name. And his trainer said if he went through with it, to get somebody else to train the horse. "I'll tell you," Wagman said, when it got to the papers, "this Cahill is a pretty popular guy."

But even if that were true, is it what I set out to be, on the terms I'd been working under? I know that every man, or many men, have jobs that affect their wives and kids. I wonder if any job outside of football, however, was like mine? Shirley and the kids could answer as well as I. Football is a continuous life. You win or lose, savor the exhilaration, or live with the regret – for maybe a day or two, and then you begin looking for the next win or loss. The day the season ends, the next one begins. Like the pianist who has forgotten how to end playing Raindrops Are Falling on My Head and therefore keeps right on playing it over and over, there is no way to finish. You're only as good as your next game. The family knows what you're working toward but they never in football get to the point where they can say, "That's it. He's done it." There's always more.

One day I was in a bowling alley. I'm a people watcher. I was watching the people bowl and trying to figure out what this guy did for a living, or that guy. I wondered what it was like to have a regular Tuesday or Wednesday night thing, to get together with a bunch of guys and bowl, and nobody knows who you are, or cares. I wondered if they were happy doing it. It's a whole different world that I've never experienced. Maybe I've missed a lot – and maybe always will, because as I was standing there I saw suddenly that they had noticed me, and recognized me, and were wondering why I was standing there staring at them.

Well, if any of them read this: that is why.

I wanted to write this book not only for myself, but – by putting my own record straight – to cast a little light on what all coaches face to some degree. I certainly realized when I started coaching how precarious a life it was, but still I thought there would be much more logic and much less mystery in disposing of a man's career.